DATE DUE

NOV 2 2 2010	

Praise for *Strategic Speed*

"The authors demonstrate in no uncertain terms that achieving strategic speed means much more than being fast. Companies that get it right place tremendous importance on employee engagement, innovation, high performance, and continuous learning at every level of the organization. By acting with clarity and purpose, they not only achieve value more quickly, they increase value over time. I urge executives everywhere to read this book. It's filled with valuable insights and actionable best practices that every company will benefit from."

—Douglas Anderson, President and CEO, Carlson Wagonlit Travel

"I thoroughly enjoyed this book. *Strategic Speed* is that rare combination of the accessible and the useful. It provides straightforward and eminently practical advice gleaned from the authors' combined seventy-five years of consulting experience. Davis, Frechette, and Boswell make things just as Einstein requested: simple, without being simplified. They identify predictable change management traps and provide useful frameworks for avoiding them."

—Amy C. Edmondson, Novartis Professor of Leadership and Management, Harvard Business School

"Where urgency meets execution. This book helps leaders tackle their greatest challenge: turning plans into action, fast. It convinced me that companies don't need to invest millions in new technology or reorganize in order to move faster and compete more aggressively; they need to tap the hidden power of their people. The authors explain in straightforward terms how to do it."

—Walt Macnee, President, International Markets, MasterCard Worldwide

"Davis, Frechette, and Boswell have put their collective finger on a huge challenge for leaders: Now that you've got a great strategy, how do you make sure your people buy in to it and bring it to life? The magic is in the execution. *Strategic Speed* provides relevant business cases and practical suggestions to create that magic and deliver real outcomes."

—Catriona Noble, Managing Director, McDonald's Australia

"A refreshing new view on strategy: how leaders can execute strategy through people, and what makes some companies faster and more agile than others. I particularly enjoyed the insights from real organizations—both the how to's and the don't do's."

—Isobel Peck, Chief Marketing Officer, Informa

"We all know that speed is a source of competitive advantage—the legions of failed efforts are ample evidence that we simply don't know how to achieve it! In *Strategic Speed*, we finally get the implementation model that needs to go with the strategy—and not a moment too soon. Bravo!"

—Len Schlesinger, President, Babson College

"The authors' concept of 'second-generation speed' is an extremely valuable leadership imperative for winning on the global playing field. The framework, case examples, and tools equip leaders to embrace and execute strategic speed."

—Noel Tichy, professor and Director, Global Citizenship Initiative at the University of Michigan; and coauthor (with Warren Bennis) of *Judgment*

"This book is packed with great insights and practical tools. Read it, use it, and gain strategic speed."

—Craig Wortmann, CEO, Experience LLC, and author of *What's Your Story?*

Strategic
Speed

Strategic Speed

Speed

Mobilize People,
Accelerate Execution

Jocelyn R. Davis
Henry M. Frechette, Jr.
Edwin H. Boswell

The Forum Corporation

Harvard Business Press
Boston, Massachusetts

No part of this publication may be reproduced, stored in or introduced into a
retrieval system, or transmitted, in any form, or by any means (electronic,
mechanical, photocopying, recording, or otherwise), without the prior
permission of the publisher. Requests for permission should be directed to
permissions@hbsp.harvard.edu, or mailed to Permissions, Harvard Business
School Publishing, 60 Harvard Way, Boston, Massachusetts 02163.

Library of Congress Cataloging-in-Publication Data

Davis, Jocelyn R.
    Strategic speed : mobilize people, accelerate execution / Jocelyn R. Davis,
Henry M. Frechette, Jr., Edwin H. Boswell
        p. cm.
    ISBN 978-1-4221-3152-7 (hbk. : alk. paper)   1. Labor productivity.
2. Employee motivation.   3. Industrial productivity.   4. Strategic planning.
I. Boswell, Edwin H.   II. Frechette, Henry M.   III. Title.
    HD57.D38 2010
    658.3'14—dc22

                                                            2009049020

The paper used in this publication meets the requirements of the American
National Standard for Permanence of Paper for Publications and Documents in
Libraries and Archives Z39.48-1992.

CONTENTS

PREFACE

This book is for any business leader who has felt frustrated that the work wasn't moving fast enough, that critical initiatives weren't gaining traction, or that a new strategy had stalled after the initial buzz subsided. It's for any leader who, despite all the time, money, and energy invested in a major new project, is disappointed that the outcomes have fallen short of expectations. It's for leaders who want to stop telling their people to move faster and instead start giving them the tools to do so.

Among the three of us, we've spent seventy-five years helping leaders and their teams around the world execute critical business strategies through people. None of us can remember the last time we met a leader who was happy with the speed of execution in his or her organization. When we asked one senior vice president at a client company whether she thought about speed, her reply was, "Only every second of every day."

During our years of working in the field, we've lived through a period when leaders' focus was mostly on two things: pace and process. *Pace* means offering incentives, cutting corners, or touting urgency in an effort to get people to speed up. *Process* means streamlining workplace processes and installing technologies in an effort to eliminate waste, improve quality, and reduce cycle time. While these efforts proved useful, they didn't fully answer our basic question: *What makes some companies faster and more agile than others?* As we reflected on our experience, interviewed clients, and sought out other business leaders for their insights, we began to see that it is a combination of pace + process + *people* that makes the difference. In other words, the missing ingredient is how leaders deliberately include people in their thinking and mobilize people to execute rapidly. (Can't you hear the cry that goes up: "It's the people, stupid!")

This is one of those insights you file under "E" for easy to say but not so easy to understand and apply. So we set out to discover the real keys to achieving what we call *strategic speed: mobilizing people, accelerating execution.* We conducted a major research study on how senior leaders can accelerate the execution of plans and strategies throughout their organization and sustain that speed over time. The research comprised:

- A comprehensive literature review, looking at hundreds of examples of accelerated and sluggish execution

- Eighteen in-depth case studies of organizations that successfully executed a major strategic initiative significantly faster than average (unless otherwise noted, quotations from leaders in case studies come from interviews we conducted from 2008 to 2009)

- A global survey of 343 senior leaders in fast and not-so-fast companies, designed to uncover the leadership practices and company characteristics that lead to the outcome of speed

This book is about what we discovered: how leaders must focus on three specific people factors and apply four critical leadership practices to drive strategic speed. Along the way, we conceived of a new way to measure speed, using two key metrics: reduced time to value and increased value over time. And to help people apply these concepts, we designed a series of assessments and tools that provide a road map for leaders who want to accelerate execution in their business.

We conducted this research intending to find insights for ourselves, but intending even more to find insights for the business leaders with whom we have or will have the pleasure of working. Our hope is that the conclusions we've drawn, the stories we've captured, and the tools we've developed will help you create a strategically speedy organization.

Acknowledgments

Strategic Speed is all about the people, and we want to thank the people who contributed.

First, we thank our research and writing team: Tom Atkinson, Steve Barry, and Ed Myers. They conducted case studies and interviews; designed assessments and surveys; read and summarized countless articles, books, and blogs; and drafted large sections of the manuscript, adding great insight at every turn. They were exemplars of strategic speed, and without them this book wouldn't exist.

Many others contributed to the book's contents. Marc Armbruster, Simon Fowler, Dottie McKissick, Rosie Mucklo, and Kim Slack worked on case studies and helped organize the research. Andre Alphonso, Jill Blick, Russell Miller, Carol Roby, Andrew Shapiro, and Gail Smith conducted interviews for various case studies. Carin Gendell researched and drafted the Jim Van Zoren case study. David Eaton contributed many of the ideas on the cultural aspects of speed used in appendix B. The literature review group consisted of Doug Bate, Wendy Carter, Nancy Coleman, Richard Hacker, Diana Newton, and David Ruef. Ron Bohlin conceived the Speed Matrix tool. Louise Axon helped shape our early thinking about execution and leadership. Maggie Walsh contributed her substantial research on change and strategy execution and gave us detailed feedback on the initial manuscript.

In Forum's marketing group, the team of Will Milano, Holly Gage, and Heather Crafts have worked tirelessly and creatively to promote the book and its messages. The Economist Intelligence Unit partnered with us on the Global Speed Survey; we benefited from the advice and assistance of EIU senior editor Dan Armstrong. Paradigm Learning, one of our partner firms, connected us with leaders at Regence so we could conduct that case study.

We're also indebted to Melinda Merino, executive editor at Harvard Business Press, and Kathleen Carr, associate editor, whose astute feedback and expert guidance improved the book immeasurably. They insisted on clarity and simplicity, and we're glad they did.

We especially appreciate and value the generosity of the wonderful clients and friends of Forum whose stories and examples are at the heart of this book. Our clients and their work were the inspiration for *Strategic Speed*, and they continue to inspire us every day. We are grateful for their time, candor, and insights. We also thank the many Forum employees and associates who helped us find stories of speed in organizations around the world.

Finally, we thank Matthew, Judy, and Lynne for their unswerving love and support.

—Jocelyn Davis, Henry Frechette, and Ed Boswell
The Forum Corporation

The Hazards of Speed

JIM VAN ZOREN was speeding down the highway toward his office in the early-morning darkness. The road stretched flat and straight for miles. "It's just me and the cows," he mused, as he pressed the accelerator of his Lexus GS10. He still missed the challenging curves of the northeastern parkways that he had driven for fifteen years in his last corporate assignment. It was only a year ago that he had accepted the position of chief information officer at SmartCom, a large, midwestern U.S. telecommunications company. SmartCom's CEO, David Hopkins, had gone looking outside the company for a CIO who could shake things up. The company was struggling to get control over its IT systems, which were a hodgepodge of new and legacy software. Van Zoren's most important task was to find and implement process reengineering opportunities, just as he had done successfully at the pharmaceutical company at which he'd previously worked. Hopkins was looking to him to deliver millions of dollars in cost efficiencies.

This morning, Van Zoren was worrying about reports on Smart-Com's billing system that he had been reviewing last night. He had staked his career on reengineering this mission-critical system, which touched all products and customers. He thought back to his first day at SmartCom, when Hopkins had given him some advice: "Jim, there are only two things that really matter in the telecom business. We have to deliver the bits and we have to bill the bits."

Van Zoren had decided nine months ago to outsource both the day-to-day management and the infrastructure development of SmartCom's vast billing system to a large, well-respected IT solutions provider, Worldwide Technology—a move that had shocked company employees and generated lots of media attention. He estimated that the outsourcing contract would save the company more than $400 million over five years. Some savings would come from reduced payroll costs, since one thousand SmartCom employees were "rebadged" as Worldwide Technology employees as part of the contract.

Van Zoren knew he had taken a big risk in outsourcing the system, and now the reports had him worried. All the IT-development projects related to the billing of new products and services were months behind schedule. Just yesterday he'd been on the phone with Shawna Rutledge, president of SmartCom's Business Customers Group; she'd been asking about the delays in the development of an electronic billing capability for some key accounts. "You know, Jim," she had said in her friendly Southern drawl, "Our customers *hate* getting their bills these days on truckloads of paper. We've been promising them electronic billing for months. What's taking so long?"

Van Zoren had been exhorting his key managers to fix the problems, but nothing had changed. Why weren't they getting the message? Did they think quality and speed were mutually exclusive? As he zoomed into his parking space at headquarters, he vowed to get some answers from his staff.

At the Staff Meeting

Van Zoren stared with exasperation at his five direct reports assembled around the conference room table. "Every week I tell you guys that we need to get our key development projects back on track, and now this latest report shows that you're falling further behind than ever," he said, waving the stapled pages in the air. "Shawna Rutledge complained to me yesterday that our big customers are getting impatient with the delays. What are you doing about this?"

The five managers looked at each other and shifted uncomfortably in their chairs. After a pause, Rob Greene, VP of systems development, spoke up. "Jim, I've been telling you since the day we signed the outsourcing contract that some of the terms are causing us problems," he said. "The biggest issue we have right now is cycle time. All the development work is being done in India. Our contract with Worldwide specifies that any help we need outside normal business hours will be charged as overtime. When we're working on a project here, the office in India is closed. Any questions on our end have to wait for about ten hours until they're back in the office, and vice versa. It slows things down. If we try to speed up a project by paying overtime, you raise issues about our overtime expenses."

Van Zoren crossed his arms and leaned back in his chair. "Rob, you've made it very clear in the past few months that you don't agree with the terms of the contract. Look, we had to move fast to get the cost savings this fiscal year, and we didn't have time to iron out every detail. Billing just doesn't have to be as complex as we've made it. It's time to find some ways to simplify the process."

Barbara Rollins, VP of data products billing, spoke up next: "But Jim, these system changes *are* complex, whether we like it or not. Our billing system started out with some off-the-shelf applications, but then we began customizing everything for our business customers. We developed specialized applications in-house and stitched them together with code that only a few people in the department know. Well, actually," she said, with a meaningful glance around the table, "they don't work *in* the department anymore." Everyone knew that these experts were among the one thousand rebadged employees who now worked for Worldwide Technology. "The problem has gotten worse recently, because some of those people have left Worldwide, and no one else knows how to write the code. I'm afraid the early systems weren't very well documented."

"Listen, Barbara," said Van Zoren, "I've heard all this before. Frankly, I think some of you are still angry about friends who lost their jobs with SmartCom. But it's time to move on, or all our jobs will be at risk. We have to find a way to get the work done and get it done *on time*. Everyone has to work faster and smarter. End of story."

Van Zoren rose from the table and clicked his laptop shut. "I have a meeting with David at ten, so I need to get going." Hearing him drop the CEO's name reminded them all that Hopkins had hand-picked Van Zoren for this job.

In the CEO's Office

Van Zoren was walking Hopkins through a spreadsheet that showed the financial results of the many process improvements he'd made. Some of his early wins, like creating a paperless office environment and eliminating individual printers in favor of shared ones, were producing millions in savings. Hopkins looked up from the spreadsheet and smiled: "Jim, these results reinforce my belief that streamlining our processes is a key part of our strategy for success. You've got my support to go on finding these opportunities and making changes as quickly as we can."

Van Zoren nodded and, after a second's hesitation, said, "David, I hope you know how difficult it can be to implement major changes like these. Take the outsourcing contract for billing, for example. We're a bit behind on some of our development projects, and I'm getting excuses from the leaders on my team. I'm still convinced we can make it work, but I may need to make some changes in staff. I need managers who'll look for more efficient ways to do things."

"Jim, you do what you need to do," replied Hopkins. "Just be sure you don't jeopardize our contracts with our big business customers. They'll take their business somewhere else if we don't meet their needs."

"I understand," said Van Zoren, rising to go. "Believe me, David, our big customers are going to be thrilled once we *really* start moving faster."

Overheard in the Hall

Van Zoren got off the elevator on his floor. Approaching Rob Greene's office, he saw Diana Hanley leaning in the doorway, her back to him. Hanley was VP of product development in the Business Customers Group and reported to Shawna Rutledge; she and Greene had been friends for years. As Van Zoren approached, he heard Hanley saying, ". . . sounds to me like Jim told Shawna what she wants to hear. Jim always commits to fixing the problem, but then nothing changes."

Van Zoren coughed loudly as he walked up. Hanley turned around and jumped when she saw him. "Oh, hi, Jim . . . um . . . Rob and I were just talking about the projects you guys are doing for us."

"And I'm as worried as you are, Diana," said Van Zoren, disguising his irritation. "I know your customers are waiting, and it doesn't seem like it should be so hard to deliver. I've been pushing my team to get on top of these timetables." He glanced at Greene, who was gazing intently out the window.

Hanley looked Van Zoren in the eye. "It's just frustrating, Jim. When I ask your group for an estimate on development time, it never sticks. Inevitably, someone tells me on the day the thing is due that it'll take another three months. My customers don't like it. Just last week, one of our biggest customers told me that this electronic billing capability might be a factor in whether or not they renew our contract for next year."

"I hear you," said Van Zoren. "I've told my team to set aggressive deadlines. Sometimes I think people around here are too focused on getting everything 100 percent right before they'll move."

He saw Hanley look anxiously toward Greene. "Well, whatever you do," she said, "don't sacrifice accuracy for speed. I've got one customer who has a hundred and four employees who spend the entire month inspecting and analyzing our bill. We don't want to go looking for trouble." She headed off down the corridor.

The CEO's Office: Six Months Later

David Hopkins frowned and clicked "Send." The angry e-mail winged its way to his executive team. Early that morning, he had been notified that SmartCom had lost a huge account, MidAmerica Financial Services, right at renewal time. According to Shawna Rutledge, what had damaged the relationship was SmartCom's lack of responsiveness. MidAmerica had been counting on electronic billing to speed up its financial reporting, and SmartCom still hadn't delivered.

Friday Morning, Two Weeks Later

Jim Van Zoren was on his way to David Hopkins' office. He was feeling confident. A month ago, SmartCom had acquired Mobiletel, another telecom company. Van Zoren assumed that Hopkins had put this meeting on his calendar in order to finalize his appointment as CIO of the newly merged organization.

Hopkins looked up from his desk as Van Zoren walked in. "Hi, Jim. I'm glad you could make time this morning. Let's sit over here," he said, pointing to the chairs around the coffee table. Van Zoren wasn't sure, but it seemed as if his boss's normally easy manner had been replaced by some hesitancy. He sat down and felt his foot begin to jiggle nervously.

"Jim, I've had some tough decisions to make over the past few weeks as I figure out the best way to merge the SmartCom and Mobiletel executive teams. One of the toughest has been deciding who to appoint as CIO." Hopkins paused to take a sip of coffee. Van Zoren could feel his heart pounding now. "I've been impressed by how quickly you launched your reengineering efforts, and the cost savings are dramatic. But Jim . . . I told you from the beginning not to jeopardize important customer relationships. Losing the MidAmerica contract is a real blow to the company, and the key factor was their dissatisfaction with our response time to their system development needs.

"I've decided that industry expertise is more critical to this role than I originally thought. So is the ability to get things done with various groups across the company. Therefore," Hopkins said, looking directly at Van Zoren, "I'm going to appoint Bill Gleason from Mobiletel as our new CIO. I'm sorry to disappoint you with this news, but I wanted to let you know before you heard rumors from anyone else."

Van Zoren sat still in his chair, stunned. He had arrived at Hopkins' office confident about how he'd been accelerating execution at SmartCom and energized by the thought of taking on new challenges in a merged organization. Now, suddenly, he was out of a job.

That case study is based on actual events that took place at a large telecom firm in the United States around 2005. But pick any large organization, in any industry, in any region of the world—perhaps your own organization—and similar stories could be told. We've all known leaders who tried to accelerate execution and instead ended up in a ditch with wheels spinning.

Where did Jim Van Zoren go wrong? He made the not-uncommon assumption that the key to speed is—well—speed. If you want a car to go faster, you step on the accelerator. If it doesn't go fast enough, you'll probably ask a mechanic to look at it and fix something: replace a part, tune the engine, or check the fuel injection. A surprising number of leaders bring this same mechanistic mind-set to the workplace (although it may be disguised in more sophisticated terms such as "the burning platform," "process reengineering," or "enterprise resource planning"): line everything up in the right order, get rid of inefficiencies, and set the speed dial to *high*. That kind of thinking got Van Zoren into trouble, and we've seen it get many others into trouble as well.

But some leaders and companies take a different approach; they manage to achieve great speed and stay out of the ditches. What's their secret?

ONE

Speed: A New View

VIRTUALLY ALL EXECUTIVES would agree that speed is necessary to a successful business. *Strategic speed* is where urgency
meets execution; it's about implementing plans and strategies not
only quickly, but well. It's something leaders pursue every day and
something they are paid to achieve.

On top of speed's intuitive appeal, our research shows a hard link
between speed and business results. We asked hundreds of leaders
from around the world to rate their company's overall speed of execution relative to others in their industry; roughly half described
their company as "faster" or "much faster." We then compared these
faster companies with those rated slower, looking at their business
performance during the previous three years. It turned out that the
faster companies had an average of 40 percent higher sales growth
and 52 percent higher operating profit than the slower companies. So
leaders are right to seek speed; it leads to positive business outcomes.

Unfortunately, speed is difficult to achieve. We don't know of
a single leader who is fully satisfied with the speed of execution

within his or her organization or team. Again, research indicates that leaders are right to be dissatisfied: study after study has shown that, on average, organizations abandon 50 to 70 percent of strategies because they fail to take hold in the organization or fail to achieve the desired results in the time expected.[1] In other words, only 30 percent of strategic initiatives fully succeed on time. This is true across all types of initiatives, from the implementation of new technology to product introductions to large organizational transformations.[2]

Given leaders' interest in speed and the difficulty of achieving it, you'd think the phenomenon would have been studied intensely—but it hasn't. It's remarkable how little agreement there is on how to achieve speed in business or on the barriers that get in the way. Many authors and consultants talk about increasing speed as if it were mostly a matter of getting in step with the times: a plethora of books and articles today exhort us all to move faster so we can keep up with the flood of information, the host of new technologies, and the rising generation of supposedly expert multitaskers. But exhortations to "hurry up" and "keep up" are of little use to leaders seeking to accelerate execution in their company or work unit. What's needed is some practical advice about speed that can be applied in a business context.

The Key to Speed

In the course of our research we discovered a surprising truth about how leaders in large organizations can accelerate execution—and a big mistake that some of those leaders are making:

- The surprising truth is that you achieve strategic speed by focusing on *people*. In other words, if you can mobilize people, you can accelerate execution. Many executives recoil from dealing with people issues because they equate them with slowing down: with having to wade through a morass of human emotions, questions, quirks, and complaints. They'd say that paying attention to people issues doesn't feel like a fast, straight road to anywhere. What we found, though, is that skillful mobilization of people is not only a help to speed but actually a key differentiator between slower and faster organizations.

- The big mistake is to pursue speed mainly by manipulating processes, systems, and technologies in a bid to become more efficient. This approach, while helpful to a degree, will get you only so far. Focusing on efficiency alone does not create speed. Though processes and technologies may appear more "manageable" than people, they're really just easier to arrange and adjust. And no matter how you arrange the mechanics of the workplace, speed will remain elusive if people issues are overlooked.

Our findings apply both to execution of large-scale initiatives (such as organizational changes, product rollouts, entry into new markets) and to execution of the myriad smaller plans and daily tasks that make up the ongoing life of an organization. We call the former *initiative execution* and the latter *everyday execution*. The good news is that leaders are in a position to accelerate both— if they pay attention to the right things.

Let's begin our investigation of speed by taking a closer look at the two specific traps into which leaders can fall. In the prologue, we saw Jim Van Zoren fall into both these traps: (1) overattention to pace, and (2) overattention to process.

Trap 1: Overattention to Pace

We've all heard the expression "Go slow to go fast," and most of us recognize the difference between doing something in a mad rush and moving at an appropriate speed. And yet when leaders are pressed to accelerate execution, their first inclination often is one of three things: to *do everything faster* (and exhort their colleagues and subordinates to do everything faster); to *stoke the boiler* by throwing more resources (money, people, or technology) at tasks and problems; or to *cut corners* by eliminating steps in a process, pieces of a project, or people in the loop. The natural reaction to a call for more speed is simply to pick up the pace.

When an organization gives too much attention to pace, you'll see these sorts of situations:

- A leader announces an important strategic initiative and stresses its urgency but fails to announce the metrics—or even basic signs—by which people will know whether progress has been made.

- A leader allows projects to be treated as fads. People pick up work with enthusiasm but then, as their initial enthusiasm wears off, they're allowed to drop that project and move on to something else.

- A leader emphasizes one particular activity over all others (such as "doing deals" or "completing customer calls in two minutes or less") and rewards people for the quantity and speed of that activity alone.

In a company caught in trap 1, people may be moving fast, they may be showing great enthusiasm, and their leaders may be handing out awards left and right—but nobody is making any real progress.

Maybe you think the examples above are obvious errors that no one would commit; surely most leaders know that simply "going fast" isn't a good idea. That might be true, were it not for the fact that "going fast" sometimes takes the shape of a sophisticated organizational program backed by corporate executives, management theories, and an enormous budget. Consider a program that once existed at General Motors called—appropriately enough—GoFast.

Rick Wagoner, then GM's president and later its CEO, started GoFast in 2000. His hope was to speed up decision making and inject a sense of urgency into the workforce. Cutting through red tape to solve problems more quickly seemed an eminently worthy goal. As Alex Taylor reported in an article for *Fortune* magazine, "The idea was simple: when negotiations over an issue reached an impasse, all the interested parties would be put together in one room until they agreed on a decision. Human resources was assigned to spread GoFast through the company. It trained GoFast coaches, arranged thousands of GoFast workshops, staged GoFast feedback sessions, and distributed GoFast coffee mugs."[3] At first, the program seemed a big success with lots of buy-in. A GM vice president of global human resources told a reporter, "Just say 'GoFast' and everyone knows what you mean."[4]

But the program soon began to sink under its own weight. By 2004, more than seven thousand GoFast meetings had been held—many for the purpose of eliminating other meetings. GoFast meetings were convened to address almost any problem or decision. "Managers," reported Taylor, "might see their performance evaluations downgraded because they weren't holding enough GoFast meetings." One executive complained, "The whole premise of GoFast became going slow"; Fritz Henderson, Wagoner's successor as CEO, said, "It wasn't helpful for decision making." In the end, it became clear that the single idea behind GoFast was just that: go fast. And going fast in itself doesn't lead to accelerated execution. The program continues within GM in a few regions of the world, and some senior leaders have adapted it to be an effective tool within their business unit. As an organization-wide mandate, however, the GoFast program ended up as a paean to pace and not much else.

Trap 2: Overattention to Process

At any university, you'll see paved walkways connecting the campus buildings to one another. You'll also see well-trodden footpaths cutting across the lawns—especially from the dormitories to the dining halls. These paths tell a story that one could call "people trump process." The architects who design campuses work out exactly where people *should* walk. But students walk where they want to go, often ignoring the walkways altogether. Strict attention to process—in this case, putting down the concrete where it's assumed people ought to walk—tends not to work. It's not that seeking to optimize processes is bad. But if you're dealing with people versus process, people will trump process every time. People will cut across the lawn if it suits them.

The same holds true in business. It's common for leaders to focus on process and, like Jim Van Zoren, pay less attention to what motivates people. Some organizations, for example, will expend a lot of effort and money installing performance management systems: complex software applications and forms intended to standardize the process of goal setting and performance appraisals. We all know of managers who treat these meetings as a matter of getting through the checklist rather than focusing on the human being in front of them. The system, disconnected from people's beliefs and behaviors, doesn't add much value.

An example of overattention to process comes from Regence, a not-for-profit U.S. health insurance company encompassing four Blue Cross Blue Shield plans in Oregon, Washington, Utah, and Idaho. The company has sixty-eight hundred employees serving approximately three million members through its health plans. During the early 2000s, Regence launched a project called REMAC (Regence Membership and Claims)—an attempt to create a shared IT system. Because a major business reason for affiliating the four

Blue Cross Blue Shield health plans was to reap efficiencies, the success of this project was critical for the new company. But the project was failing. REMAC involved an enormous amount of effort but didn't resolve a core dilemma: the company still had four sets of products, business plans, and fiduciary boards—as well as four very different business cultures. Years of work on REMAC focused on integrating technologies and processes but ignored the people issues that the company's employees faced on a day-to-day basis. Once Regence started addressing the people issues, however—as we'll describe later—the company became an inspiring example of speed.

To be sure, efficient processes and technologies are helpful to speed, and efforts to improve them aren't missteps; they can definitely add value. But such process-focused efforts to increase speed don't go far enough. Without equal or greater attention to people factors, leaders' efforts to improve processes and technologies are at best insufficient; at worst detrimental. As the biologist Lewis Thomas once said, "If you want a bee to make honey, you do not issue protocols on solar navigation or carbohydrate chemistry; you put him together with other bees."

Faster Companies Attend to People Factors

As part of our Global Speed Survey, we asked the leaders to rate their company's overall speed of strategy execution in relation to other companies in their industry. We then validated the leaders' perceptions against publicly available data on company metrics, thereby obtaining a pool of faster companies and a pool of slower companies that we could compare. (See appendix A for a full description of the Global Speed Survey findings.)

Among other questions, we asked the respondents to think about a strategic initiative in their company that was executed quickly and successfully, and we asked them about the characteristics of that initiative and of the teams and organizational structures that affected it. We also asked them to think about their organization as a whole and its typical practices. For each question, we essentially asked, "Was the initiative (or is your organization) more like A or more like B?" We then compared the pattern of responses in the faster companies with those in the slower companies. This forced-choice mechanism allowed us to tease out the differences in how leaders in faster and slower companies tend to approach execution.

We were surprised at the findings. On ten out of twelve items, the responses of the leaders in faster companies were strikingly different from those of leaders in the slower companies (see table 1-1).

What emerges is a picture of two very different approaches to strategy execution, management, and daily work:

- In the *slower companies*, the emphasis is on efficiency, keeping up the pace, sticking with the known, staying focused on one's own work, and not worrying too much about alignment.

- In the *faster companies*, the emphasis is on alignment, flexibility, openness, innovative thinking, and taking the time to reflect and learn.

Of course, most leaders know on some level that the approaches shown in the left column of table 1-1 are good things to do, and many pay lip service to those practices in the name of "boosting morale" or "increasing employee engagement." What we find striking, though, is that the left-column approaches actually predict the *speed of execution* in a company. And, as we saw earlier, speed of execution predicts hard business results such as increases in sales growth and operating profit.

TABLE 1-1

Differences between faster and slower companies

Leaders tended to describe successful initiatives and their company as having the following characteristics:

Faster, more successful companies	Slower, less successful companies
1. Senior leaders are closely aligned and committed to the success of initiatives.	1. Initiatives succeed in spite of lack of unanimous senior level support.
2. Team members are flexible about switching responsibilities to make things easier for one another.	2. Team members stay focused on their responsibilities to ensure the work gets done.
3. Team members are usually comfortable talking about problems and disagreements.	3. Team members believe in keeping their cards close to the vest as the best way to get ahead.
4. Despite the workload, people on initiative teams find time to review how the work is going.	4. There is simply no time for reflection among initiative teams.
5. Teams capture and communicate lessons learned from initiatives.	5. After initiatives, teams move on to other assignments without a formal debrief.
6. The company bases its success on the ability to explore new technologies.	6. The company bases its success on the ability to improve quality and lower costs.
7. The company creates products and services that are innovative.	7. The company fine-tunes what it offers to keep its current customers satisfied.
8. Management systems work coherently to support overall objectives.	8. People often work at cross-purposes because management systems give them competing objectives.
9. When making important decisions that affect the company's future, senior leaders usually put forward creative and innovative ideas.	9. When making important decisions that affect the company's future, senior leaders usually put forward tried and true ideas.
10. Even experienced employees in this company receive training when new initiatives are launched.	10. We rarely have time for training and education around new initiatives in this company.

Many leaders assume there's a trade-off between speed and engagement, speed and learning, speed and alignment: when you want to go fast, there just isn't time for all that "people stuff," especially in less "people-oriented" environments (see "Is This Just About 'Knowledge Work'?"). This data suggests that, on the contrary, leaders can actually increase speed of execution by adopting some practices that don't appear to focus on speed.

IS THIS JUST ABOUT "KNOWLEDGE WORK"?

It's easy to see how important the people issues are to achieving speed in knowledge work environments, which are essentially complex, collaborative, and relationship-oriented rather than oriented toward routine tasks. Jobs that focus on "tacit" interactions (those that require a high level of judgment and applied knowledge), as opposed to "transactional" interactions, now make up 25 to 50 percent of jobs in developed nations.[a] The number of these types of jobs is increasing faster than any other. For managers, salespeople, software engineers, financial advisers, film producers, insurance agents, and teachers, productivity isn't about doing rote tasks more efficiently; it's about increasing judgment, collaboration, and innovation. In medicine, for example, speed depends largely on the ability of physicians, nurses, and administrators to build trusting relationships with patients and colleagues, to access better information, to learn from every case, and a host of other intangibles.

But even in manufacturing environments—where one might think success depends heavily on efficient processes and technologies—the benefits of process improvements are elusive. A study by Michael Lapré and Luk Van Wassenhove published

Vodafone Group: Relying on Pace, Process, and—Most of All—People

Although Jim Van Zoren's company stumbled, the telecom industry can boast some fine examples of speed. Vodafone Group Plc is one of the world's leading mobile telecommunications companies, with a presence in Europe, the Middle East, Africa, Asia Pacific, and the United States (through Verizon Wireless). With a vision of being

---

in *Harvard Business Review* looked at sixty-two process improvement projects throughout the 1980s and 1990s in one manufacturing plant of the Belgian company Bekaert, the world's largest maker of steel wire. Of all the projects, "only about 25% delivered factory-wide improvements. Half had no bottom-line impact whatsoever, and, even more surprising, the remaining 25% had a negative impact on the plant's overall productivity improvement."[b]

The common characteristic of the successful projects? A focus on *learning*. Specifically, when members of a project team saw their charter as primarily about creating new, reliable knowledge and transferring that knowledge broadly to other groups across the factory, the project was successful in enhancing productivity. Those projects with a focus on efficiency alone, or where learning was narrowly confined to one team or area, had no impact or a *negative* impact on productivity. So, even in manufacturing, achievement of speed hinges on people factors.

a. Scott C. Beardsley, Bradford C. Johnson, and James M. Manyika, "Competitive Advantage from Better Interactions," *McKinsey Quarterly*, no. 2 (2006): 53–63.

b. Michael A. Lapré and Luk N. Van Wassenhove, "Learning Across Lines: The Secret to More Efficient Factories," *Harvard Business Review*, October 2002, 107–111.

"the communications leader in an increasingly connected world," Vodafone Group has more than 300 million customers and offers a spectrum of services that include voice, data, and devices for consumers and businesses. The company has become famous for speed of expansion—mostly through acquisitions—and speed of execution. "In this industry, an organization that is sluggish will not be successful," says chief executive Vittorio Colao. "There is quite fearsome competition, and you have to be very flexible and nimble."

For this reason, Colao has made speed one of the strategic cornerstones of the business. He explains:

> The three key words for us are speed, simplicity, and trust—which in a way correspond to pace, process, and people. Pace is the pure speed element. Process is something you have to pay attention to in a large company, but it's something you need to simplify as much as possible. Then there's people, which we'd put under the "trust" category, because if you want people to move fast and simplify processes, the key is to inject a high degree of trust. People must know that risk taking and judgment calls are fine; they must have trust in one another. Trust is also the glue that holds different functions and processes together.

Colao has put his finger on the three pieces of the speed puzzle and a main reason why it's the people element that's the largest and most critical piece. In order to act quickly and efficiently, people need to have *confidence in themselves and in their leaders*: they need to know where they're heading and why; they need to feel they can make judgment calls and course corrections in the moment; and they need to trust that their managers and colleagues are going to back them up, not trip them up. Says Colao, "Every company talks a lot about speed and moving quickly, but if you don't have trust, people will say, 'You ask me to be fast, but at the end of the day, if I make a mistake I'll be killed.'" When human beings are scared, their tendency is not to press forward but to freeze in place (or to move very, very slowly).

In short, speed in organizations depends on pace, process, and people, but it's the people factors that turn out to be the most powerful accelerator—or brake. As a leader, you can have all the processes and technologies in place, all the charts and graphs drawn up, all the money in hand, and all the angels on your side . . . but if the people won't move, the work won't move.

Focus on People: The Three Most Important Factors

Leaders, however, need more specific guidance than just "Focus on people factors." Which people factors are we talking about?

Our research indicates that there are three conditions that effective leaders in fast organizations seek to increase, and that in turn increase strategic speed:

- Clarity: Shared, clear understanding of your situation and direction

- Unity: Wholehearted agreement on the merits of that direction and the need to work together to move ahead

- Agility: Willingness to turn and adapt quickly while keeping strategic goals in mind

Clarity, unity, and agility are what leaders need to aim for in order to increase speed. The metaphor we often use with our client firms is elite sprinters: the men and women who compete at Olympic levels in the 100-, 200-, and 400-meter dashes. Of course they train rigorously so they can run fast, but during a race, they're not thinking, "Run fast." Quite the opposite: they're thinking, "Relax." In order to achieve an outcome, it's not always a good idea to aim for that outcome. Elite runners *aim* to relax, and the *result* is greater speed. Similarly, to achieve speed in business, you need to focus on something other than speed itself; you need to focus on clarity, unity, and agility. Let's take a closer look at each factor.

Clarity. Clarity includes the following items from our survey (see table 1-1):

- Senior leaders are closely aligned and committed.

- People find time to review how the work is going.

- Teams capture and communicate lessons learned.

- Employees receive training when new initiatives are launched.

Our case studies highlighted some additional facets of clarity. For example, we found that clarity doesn't come from making one clear announcement, nor does it come from repeating that announcement many times. Rather, clarity is a result of two-way conversations in which people have a chance to ask questions, discuss, and learn. We also found that clarity isn't just about having a clear sense of the destination; it's also about being able to perceive the road you're on, the potholes in that road, how far you've come, and how far you have to go. It's about seeing clearly throughout the entire journey. Clarity means having the *vision* to go fast.

Unity. Unity includes these items from our survey:

- Senior leaders are closely aligned and committed.

- Team members are flexible about switching responsibilities to make things easier for one another.

- Team members are comfortable talking about problems and disagreements.

- Management systems work coherently to support overall objectives.

Again, we found that the leaders in our case studies talked about unity in some interesting ways. First, unity is not just about your immediate team. Much has been written about functional versus dysfunctional teams, and teamwork is certainly one aspect of unity. Equally as important, though, is the ability to develop unity with stakeholders across your company and even outside your company. Unity is about cross-boundary collaboration, not just collaboration with teammates. Second, unity requires not only approving of a goal but also having the skills and the will to do the tasks required, to keep going over the long haul, and to work effectively and cheerfully with others, all in service of the goal. In other words, unity means having the *strength* to go fast.

Agility. Agility includes these items from our survey:

- The company bases its success on the ability to explore new technologies and methods.

- The company creates products and services that are innovative.

- When making important decisions, senior leaders usually put forward creative and innovative ideas.

You won't be surprised to hear that we don't believe agility hinges on setting up particular kinds of organizational structures or processes (though many consultants talk about agility that way). Although processes can be more or less restrictive, no process is in itself agile. As a leader we know once said, "People are the only asset that innovates." Another thing you'll read in many management books is that agility equals awareness; it's described as a matter of sensing changes in the environment and noticing stumbling blocks that could affect your plans. "Sensing" and "noticing" are indeed important, but we found that they aren't the big challenges for most leaders. Most people have no trouble noticing changes and stumbling blocks. They do have trouble, however, with being willing and able to adjust course *after* noticing. Agility, in most cases, means having the *flexibility* to go fast.

So one way to grasp the essence of these three people factors is to compare them to physical characteristics: vision, strength, and flexibility. Here's another way to understand them: if a leader succeeds in fostering clarity, unity, and agility, the members of his or her organization or team will tend to answer *yes* to three questions:

- Do I know where we're going and why? (clarity)

- Am I committed to working with these people to get there? (unity)

- Am I willing to suggest and try many different ways to get there? (agility)

One more point: the order in which you address the factors matters. Clarity must come first. Unity is built on a foundation of clarity. And true agility is impossible without clarity and unity. When we explore the three people factors in chapter 2, we'll show in more detail how they build upon each other.

Measuring Speed: Focus on Value

Frank Gilbreth, a pioneer of scientific management methods in the early 1900s, found that he could reduce the time it took him to shave by one minute if he used two razors at once. He gave up on the idea when he noticed that it took him two additional minutes to bandage the wounds. Gilbreth might have summarized thus: If your efforts to boost speed create mangled results, you haven't really boosted speed at all.

We spoke earlier about the two traps into which leaders often fall when they try to accelerate execution: overattention to pace and overattention to process. But there's one more mistake leaders make, and it may be the most fundamental one: they measure speed in their organization as if it were nothing more than a race. They think, "How fast can we get from A to B?" (For Gilbreth it was: "How fast can I shave?") This mind-set puts pace and process at the forefront of their concerns and causes them to overlook an essential component of strategic speed: *value*.

We've reviewed many assessments of organizational speed and agility, and one of their commonalities is that they assess speed mostly in terms of pace: how quickly tasks, projects, and initiatives get done, how rapidly the organization reacts to external events, or how often deadlines are met. What they miss is the question of whether any value is being created amid all the activity. If strategies, projects, teams, and individuals aren't adding value to the organization and its constituents, they aren't really moving forward at all; they're only spinning in place. If leaders don't incorporate value into how they think about speed and how they measure it, they're unlikely to make any real progress toward accelerating execution. Therefore, we'd like to offer a new way to size up speed.

New Metrics for Speed: Time to Value and Value over Time

In any organization there are always some initiatives or projects with clear beginning and end points, and those may feel very much like races to a finish line, especially if they have strict deadlines. In many other cases, though, there is no finish line. Where is the finish line for a sales team trying to make their numbers month after month? For an R&D director's mission to develop new products more quickly? Or for an entire organization's attempt to stay ahead of the competition by implementing a new strategy? Speeding up in these and many other situations doesn't mean getting from A to B fast. Instead, it means shortening the time it takes for people and initiatives to add value to the enterprise.

Think about a job or role that you held for at least several years. Now think back to when you were new to that job or role. Most likely, you were well-suited to the job, possessed of the right skills, and eager to make a difference on day one. But as you look back from today's vantage point, how long did it take for you to add enough value to the enterprise to outweigh the effort it took for your managers and colleagues to train and acculturate you? Six months? A year? It's commonplace in most industries that the cost of replacing an employee is one to two times that employee's annual salary. A large part of that cost is the time and effort it takes to get employees to the point where they're pulling their own weight rather than weighing down the enterprise. Similarly, work projects typically take two or three times longer than expected before they begin contributing real value to the enterprise. At its start, and often for a long time after that, a project does little more than suck up resources and create noise in the system. New teams make 50 percent more mistakes than established teams do, and more than half those mistakes occur in the course of their first efforts together.[5]

You may have hired brilliant employees and conceived brilliant strategies, but unless you can reduce the time it takes for employees, leaders, teams, or initiatives *to contribute to the enterprise in the manner and to the extent that they were meant to contribute*— and then ensure that they *continue* to contribute—you won't really be accelerating execution.

The leaders in our case studies measure strategic speed not in terms of races won, but in terms of two broader metrics: *reduced time to value* and *increased value over time* (see figure 1-1).

Time to value is the time it takes for people or initiatives to climb above the line or point at which they start contributing net value to the system rather than being a net hindrance. *Value over time* is the value created as they *stay* above the line. We call the horizontal axis the *noise-value line*, because when people or initiatives fail to climb above it, they are sources mainly of noise (distractions and static) as opposed to value (productivity and progress). Take a look at figures 1-2 and 1-3; each represents a different scenario for the noise-value line.

Figure 1-2 (long time to value; little value over time) is the worst-case scenario. Figure 1-3 (short time to value; substantial value over time) is the best-case scenario. You can imagine other

FIGURE 1-1

Measuring strategic speed

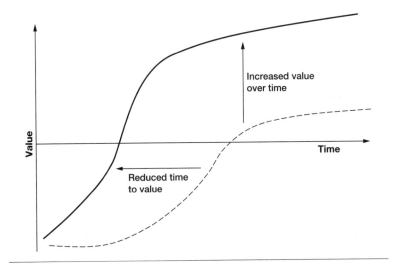

FIGURE 1-2

Long time to value, little value over time

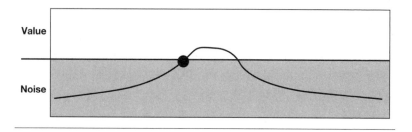

FIGURE 1-3

Short time to value, substantial value over time

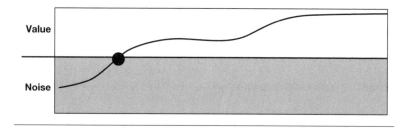

scenarios: for example, one where time to value is short (good), but value over time drops off quickly (bad); or one where time to value is long (bad), but value over time stays high (good). In chapter 7, you'll find a Time/Value Assessment tool that lets you create noise-value charts by which you can track time to value and value over time within your business unit.

SunGard: Reducing Time to Value

Though on-boarding is by no means the only situation in which reducing time to value is critical, getting people up to speed when they step into new or redesigned roles is one of the most familiar instances where this metric applies. SunGard, an IT services company, reduced time to value when their leaders launched a new telemarketing unit.

SunGard, an acronym for Sun Guaranteed Access to Recovered Data, is a privately held *Fortune* 500 company that serves organizations in the financial, higher education, and public sectors. In 2007, senior management were looking to grow SunGard's Availability Services business, which protects companies' business operations from such threats as security breaches, network or power failures, and extreme events ranging from natural disasters to terrorist attacks. It originated as a disaster recovery service, where SunGard played a more limited role in protecting or restoring clients' data. The new strategy was for Availability Services to be a leader in managed services, which involved taking greater responsibility for maintaining the client's data operations on a day-to-day basis. The sales force, however, was a major impediment. Its people were ill-prepared to function in a managed-services world; they were transactional, reactive, and accustomed to having full autonomy to close deals with little accountability.

To address this problem, John Cooper was brought on board as the company's executive vice president of North American sales. To begin the transformation of the sales organization, Cooper put in place a new set of core sales models and processes. This necessitated retraining the entire sales force and sometimes making sweeping changes in personnel. One project in particular is an excellent example of reduced time to value. Salespeople in SunGard's newly formed telemarketing channel needed to be brought up to speed quickly both on telemarketing skills and on the new sales model. In response, Jim Olson, SVP of sales support, devised a new coaching process. Instead of undergoing months of training before they began making calls (a typical practice), salespeople were put on the floor, making calls, as soon as they came on board. The new process—dubbed "sell/coach/sell/coach"—entailed observing the salespeople on the phone, coaching them immediately after each call, and having them make another call. At first, Olson and his team found that while the salespeople could learn fairly quickly to conduct a call effectively, they had trouble closing. But they persisted with the "sell/coach" approach until the new hires became skilled at closing, as well—in record time. What had been a six-month process of getting salespeople into the field became a much quicker method for achieving full-fledged sales results among new members of the team.

SunGard: Increasing Value over Time

Value over time is the ability to stay above the noise-value line. Sometimes an individual, team, or initiative quickly begins to add value but, later, keeps slipping back down into the noise zone, becoming more of a hindrance or distraction than a help to the enterprise.

If your organization has a lot of people who are dashing to and fro but who can't stay above the noise-value line, all they're really doing is creating drag on the entire organization. If value isn't being created, it doesn't matter how fast a particular individual, team, or project is moving—the net effect is to slow the system down. It's like trying to cross a lake in a speedboat with several propellers, all spinning at top speed but aimed in different directions. The individual propellers are indeed going fast, but as a group they're making it awfully hard for the speedboat to move forward at all.

We saw how John Cooper and Jim Olson reduced time to value when SunGard launched a new sales model and a new telemarketing channel. But Cooper faced an even larger challenge, and, in meeting it, increased value over time.

A few years earlier, SunGard had outbid Hewlett-Packard for the purchase of Comdisco's computer services operations. This acquisition had doubled the size of the company and of the sales force.

When Cooper joined SunGard, he found a sales force practicing a wide array of approaches. As he puts it, "You could do it the Comdisco way, or do it the SunGard way, or do it some other way." Cooper moved quickly to create a uniform approach to serving customers and encourage greater collaboration across functions. Everyone in the organization—whether in sales, engineering, marketing, or operations—was now held accountable for sales, service, and client retention. Engineers would go on sales calls and build relationships with clients. Salespeople, able to make smooth handoffs to the service function, spent much less time with customers after making a sale, which enabled them to make more sales. Post-sale issues were handled faster and more flexibly. These changes had almost immediate results, as the sales force identified at least $3 million in increased revenue within one year of the merger. In addition, retention of salespeople increased 50 percent over three years. By getting all the "propellers" aligned and working smoothly together, Cooper helped lift the merged sales forces above the noise-value line and increased value over time.

As long as leaders fail to attend to people factors and fail to incorporate value into their ideas about speed, the best they'll ever achieve is superficial speed: lots of activity, little forward motion. Jim Van Zoren's approach to execution—lining everything up in a logical manner, removing inefficiencies, and setting the speed dial to *high*—overlooks not only the central role of people, but also the fact that speed isn't really speed unless it's creating value.

TWO

The People Factors:
Clarity, Unity, Agility

IN THIS CHAPTER, we'll take a closer look at each of the three
people factors that drive speed and explore some examples of
how companies have succeeded—or failed—at managing them.
We'll then present a Strategic Speedometer tool that allows you to
see how you're doing on the three factors in comparison to other
companies, and we'll look at some common organizational patterns
that result when people factors are missing or out of balance. Finally,
we'll introduce four specific leadership practices that are your reliable levers for boosting clarity, unity, and agility.

Clarity

Senior managers spend a lot of time striving to increase the clarity of
their strategies. They work with their leadership teams to identify
market opportunities and customer requirements; assess competitive

threats and how to avert them; size up their organizational capabilities; and determine where to make investments in capital equipment and people. They write up strategy documents and launch communication campaigns. Yet, though the strategy is often 100 percent clear in the mind of the leader or among the senior leadership team, they're often frustrated by the lack of clarity throughout the company. How many times have you grumbled, "I've explained this goal [strategy, initiative, project] a hundred times, and people *still* don't get it!"

Clarity means your people can confidently answer the question, "Where are we going and why?" They should also be able to answer three other questions:

- What are the external conditions we face?

- What are our internal capabilities?

- Based on all these factors, what should we do—and how should we act?

Note that it's far more important for your employees to be able to answer those questions than for you, the leader, to be able to answer them. In the case studies we conducted, we found that effective leaders spent relatively little time seeking clarity on their own and a lot of time working with their employees to develop a clear picture together.

We'll begin our look at clarity with the story of a company where senior managers are perfectly clear about their strategy—but nobody else is.

Airux Corporation: Repetition Without Clarity

Airux Corporation (the name and industry have been changed) is a global organization that manufactures packaging and containers. The firm has grown chiefly through acquisitions. During the expansion, executives have done little to inculcate a uniform culture or corporate strategy; they have simply acquired companies and then either set them up as subsidiaries or merged them with other acquisitions. Now management is attempting to change the strategy and culture so that Airux can become faster and more innovative.

The company's most recent initiative, "Reach," is a leadership development program focusing on four attributes: strategy, innovation, globalization, and learning. The people selected to participate are all senior leaders—the next generation of top leadership within the firm. Though its goals are worthy, the Reach initiative has been problematic from the start. The main problem is that the program hasn't been communicated clearly to its audience. Ironically, if you ask the people in charge of running the program, they say that Reach may even have been overcommunicated; yet if you ask the program's participants how *they* perceive it, many express puzzlement and frustration. They say things such as: "We get all these memos, but I still don't understand what's going on," and "This program sounds kind of cool, but why exactly are we doing it?" Despite a huge investment of time, money, and effort, the people in charge of Reach haven't managed to convey its purpose and desired outcomes.

Why has the message failed to get through? Top management have communicated the message over and over again, and they insist that they've been clear. As we step back, however, and look beyond the constant e-mails and announcements, we see a larger problem: the new attributes that Reach is meant to inculcate—strategy, innovation, globalization, and learning—are at odds with the company's deal-making culture. To many leaders down the ranks, it feels as if senior management is trying to bolt on some some qualities very much at odds with a financially driven, cost-conscious mind-set. The messages are mixed, and occasionally they seem downright contradictory. In addition, although top managers have explained the new strategy hundreds of times, they haven't explained it in a compelling or engaging way. As a result, leaders don't understand why Reach is important or how they might benefit from it. As one person said, "It seems as if we're just being asked to do a lot more work for no good reason."

Executives at Airux have mistaken repetition for clarity. To achieve true clarity around Reach, they will need to do more than keep hammering away at the same points. They'll need to: (1) resolve the mixed messages by acknowledging the current deal-making culture and showing how the elements of Reach will help change that culture; (2) make a compelling case for the Reach goals, showing why achieving those goals is critical to the business and beneficial to Airux leaders and employees; and (3) help their people know the answers to the three critical questions posed above: What are the external conditions we face? What are our internal capabilities? Based on all these factors, how should we act?

Some leaders are doing all the right things when it comes to creating clarity, but something very mundane gets in their way: clutter. Whether you're navigating an ocean concealing icebergs, a sea of unnecessary reports, or an overwhelming product set, it does no good simply to forge ahead and hope you won't hit anything. It doesn't matter how clear you've been about the destination; if your people have to pick their way through clutter every day, they can't see where they're going. (Recall that clarity means having the *vision* to go fast.) Clearing clutter is one of the easiest ways to increase the volume and clarity of your strategic messages. If you feel you've done all the right things, yet your employees still don't understand where they're headed and why, consider doing some basic housecleaning—as Kirk Kimler, a leader at Thermo Fisher Scientific, did to great effect.

Thermo Fisher Scientific: Clearing the Clutter

With annual revenues of over $10 billion, Thermo Fisher Scientific sells high-end analytical instruments as well as laboratory equipment, chemicals, supplies, software, and services. Fisher HealthCare, the health care market division of the company, offers a thick catalogue of more than 600,000 clinical products, ranging from disposable rubber gloves and syringes to state-of-the-art pieces of lab equipment valued at several hundred thousand dollars. On the low end, Fisher was selling short-term consumables, which had a simple, quick-turnaround sales cycle. On the high end, its sales process was much more complex. For both types of sales situations, Fisher faced strongly established competitors.

Kirk Kimler, the head of marketing for Fisher HealthCare, devised a marketing plan for the organization that would standardize the sales process and create a product mix that would steady sales and provide Fisher with long-term protection from market fluctuations. He had a very clear vision of what he was trying to accomplish and of how to do it. He realized that in order to make the transition, he had to get the sales force to think and work differently.

As a first step, we helped the Fisher sales force understand Kimler's plan and figure out what they needed to do in response. A two-day-long intervention was attended by a cross-section of the organization, including executives, sales leaders, marketing staff, and the head of HR. Kimler kicked off the event, briefly reiterating the strategic plan and reminding the group of why this work was so important. Then—instead of more explanation of the plan via a slew of presentations—the session proceeded with "spring cleaning."

Managers had been asked to bring in a copy of every type of report they touched, filled out, or read. They produced seventy-three. The mentality was, "I'm in charge of chemical reagents; I want you to fill out my Chemical Reagent Call Report, because even though nobody else uses it, it's what I use to do my work." The reports said little about the desired outcomes of anyone's work, nor did they match with how the sales process worked from initial prospecting to close. At the end of two days, the group had discarded all but twenty reports. As the initiative went forward, Kimler further streamlined the sales process and reduced paperwork.

By end of the year, Kimler was president of Fisher HealthCare. He undertook many other initiatives to increase the speed of the organization, yet nothing was ever more important than clarifying priorities and streamlining the work. In his management meetings, he would regularly ask leaders to prioritize the ten most important things they needed to do and get rid of everything else. Kimler refers to this as "lowering the water in the system so they're able to see the rocks." (Interestingly, Vodafone chief executive Vittorio Colao uses a similar metaphor when he talks about the need to simplify. People in large companies, he says, often become frustrated with their complexity and resulting slowness. He compares it to hiking through beautiful country "with a big backpack full of rocks on your back.")

Unity

Unity means that once people are clear on where they're headed, they agree wholeheartedly on the merits of that direction and the need to work together to move ahead. Unity is perhaps the least-appreciated factor of speed. Executives often understand that if they want plans and strategies executed more quickly, they need to set clear direction, create a sense of urgency, reduce bureaucratic delays, and adapt nimbly to changing conditions. What they often don't see is the extent to which lack of unity within teams, across the organization, and with external stakeholders tends to undermine everyone's best efforts to move quickly.

In business, collaboration is the main driver of unity. When leaders foster a culture of collaboration, spell out a common cause, and ensure that everyone is equipped with the necessary technical and soft skills to make their contributions, projects and strategies hold together. When, instead, the culture is one of internal competition, mistrust, and turf wars—or just simple unawareness of what other groups are doing—projects and strategies fall apart. Lack of collaboration and a resulting lack of unity is a chief reason for teams and initiatives sinking and staying below the noise-value line.

Fortunately, positive examples of unity aren't hard to find. We were interested to find that in several of our case studies, leaders adopted the same mechanism as part of their efforts to increase speed: when launching an initiative, they chose to bring together people from different divisions, roles, and geographies for strategy and training sessions. This was an expensive and apparently slower approach, and one to which many objected strenuously at first. In all cases, however, leaders eventually named this tactic as critical both to reducing time to value and to increasing value over time.

Waypoint: Bringing People Together

One company that took this "mix people together" approach is Waypoint LLC, an industry association of seven regional food service brokers. Waypoint was established in March 2008 with a clear mission statement—to build an organization that would help the industry reach new standards and new levels of performance. One of the first initiatives Waypoint undertook was the development of a common sales process for the seven member firms, followed by training in that process for all sales managers. To augment clarity with unity, leaders decided to mix the groups from each of several different geographical areas of the United States during sales management training, bringing participants together in multiregion sessions.

This approach cost more and prompted some participants to balk initially; however, as described by Bill Mason, a consultant at The Hale Group, who worked with Waypoint to foster this initiative:

> The mixed-region approach has been a big key to fast uptake
> of the training, because—to put it simply—all the sales

managers now talk to each other! During the training session we also mixed up the companies. On the West Coast we did a company from the Midwest plus the West Coast salespeople, and we mixed them up a little bit. Every time we ran one of these sales training sessions, I would get e-mails from various company owners saying, "You cannot believe how high the morale is in the company today. Even though we didn't have a great year and we didn't pay bonuses, we have the highest morale that we've ever had."

Intentionally bringing together people from multiple regions and functions when you launch an initiative can increase strategic speed. Despite greater initial cost, time, and complexity, this approach pays off in the end, because it creates unity—a bond and a sense of common cause—among the players.

Earlier we mentioned the importance of creating unity not just within a team, nor just within a company, but also beyond a company's boundaries. Unity within an organization is important to speed, but just as important is unity between the organization and its external stakeholders. Tata Sky—an organization with a strong focus on people factors, and one we'll revisit many times in this book—provides an excellent example of both internal and external unity.

Tata Sky: Satellite TV Rockets to Success

Tata Sky is a joint venture between the Tata Group, India's largest business conglomerate, and Star, a Hong Kong-based media and entertainment company. Tata Sky has partnered with global leaders in digital technology to bring a state-of-the-art satellite television service to India. The company launched its direct-to-home (DTH) satellite pay-TV service in August 2006 with the goal of reaching one million connections by the end of its first year of operation. It achieved that goal, and then took only another ten months to reach two million connections and just seven more months to reach three million.

As Vikram Kaushik, CEO of Tata Sky, explains, "Tata Sky was the first prepaid satellite television service ever in the world. The consumer is sold a subscription in advance for the month. Subsequently, they can either buy vouchers from ordinary shops, or they can use their credit cards or even texting on their mobile phones to charge their accounts."

Today, the Tata Sky satellite TV platform delivers nearly two hundred television channels, movies, and interactive services for games, learning, news, chat, and other applications. It has a retail network that covers more than seven thousand towns in India, with close to four million subscribers.

When the venture was only six months old, Tata Sky asked Nielsen Media Research to conduct a customer satisfaction survey. When Nielsen benchmarked them against all companies in the telecommunications and the consumer durables sectors—not just in India, but around the world—Tata Sky received the highest customer satisfaction scores. According to Nielsen, this was an amazing feat for a brand that hadn't existed just six months before. Kaushik notes, "The millions of connections we've achieved are not as important as the fact that we have been able to create the gold standard for customer service in India."

Tata Sky did not start on a level playing field. The new venture faced intense initial competition from the Zee-Essel Group, a large Indian media company. "They created a whole series of barriers to entry for us," says Kaushik. The company also faced a difficult regulatory environment in India. Confronting these challenges, it executed fast in order to succeed.

Leaders at Tata Sky worked hard to create unity not only inside the company but also with stakeholders outside the company—distributors, shop salesclerks, and journalists. Vikram Kaushik describes their approach:

> I took a leaf out of my training as a seasoned marketing person and decided we would do a formal product launch the way consumer products are launched, with a lot of excitement and conferences. To do so, we ran several of these conferences at the big centers in the north, east, and west. We invited the entire sales force, and we invited the trade—the distributors who would sell the product. We treated the trade as a part of this venture rather than saying, "You're the trade and we are the company." They participated in this whole process and were enthused and encouraged and motivated. It began like a big party. When the product was launched, we used the principles once again from consumer product marketing—merchandising the product in shops so that consumers would be curious and come to see what was happening.

Deepa Watsa, Tata Sky's chief HR officer, describes how thousands of "shop boys" were trained to demonstrate the Tata Sky product: "Demonstration became a critical part of this entire exercise. Within the first three months, the Tata Sky box was available in close to twenty-thousand shops across the country. Any consumer living anywhere could have access to go and have a look at it. That was a very important part, because otherwise people are wary of new products. The demonstration piece was crucial to our entire strategy."

Kaushik and his team also focused on interactions with influential Indian journalists:

> Six months before we launched, I identified eight very important journalists. We got them into a room and told them that

the DTH operation that had been launched in India was not satellite TV as they knew it. We wanted them to see it. I put them in a plane and flew them to Sydney and took them to Foxtel. There we showed them what a DTH operation is. After that, we flew them to Melbourne and showed them what a call center looks like—how consumer responses are dealt with and what subscriber management systems have to be put in place, the sophisticated information technology back room that has to be created, and how this whole thing is run. So when we came back, they were writing articles about how "the real DTH is going to arrive now." We created 360-degree communication, so that people were already curious about what this new Tata Sky thing was going to be and what it would offer.

The unity that Kaushik created with multiple external stakeholders—from distributors, to "shop boys," to journalists—was a key factor in how quickly Tata Sky succeeded.

Agility

Agility has become a topic of much interest in the business community. In his book *Business Agility*, Michael Hugos writes, "Most profitable opportunities in the global economy are, by definition, short-term opportunities. Companies need to respond and act quickly on opportunities that arise."[1] Jumping on opportunities is no doubt important, but our case studies suggest that agility is less a matter of adapting one's direction continuously and more a matter of being open to *different ways to achieve the direction* you have set for yourself. In other words, real agility isn't about heading north one day and east the next; that's vacillation. Agility is about heading consistently north, but being willing to use sails one day and the onboard motor the next, as conditions demand. To use another sailing metaphor, some leaders react to an ill wind by saying, "The wind is against us; we'd better change course" (vacillation), when they would do better to say, "The wind is against us, so let's start tacking so we can keep moving forward" (agility).

We define agility as the willingness to turn and adapt quickly while keeping strategic goals in mind. Here's a story that illustrates what we mean.

The American University of Iraq: *Agility in Higher Learning*

When agility is high, people are prepared to improvise. Nowhere is a spirit of improvisation more apparent than at the American University of Iraq.

Imagine setting out to build an entire university from scratch. Now imagine doing it in a war zone. That was the vision of John Agresto, who believes that the path to lasting peace starts with education. Agresto, a former university president, has been working since 2003 to collaborate with Iraqi government officials, American professors, and Iraqi and American donors to found a private university in Sulaimaniya, a city in the Kurdish area of northern Iraq. They have a remarkable goal: to establish a fully functioning, five-thousand-student university within just five to six years. This daunting project has required Agresto and his colleagues to use unconventional approaches and to make fast course corrections. As Agresto describes the situation, "The model has to be: if at first you don't succeed, screw it. Try something else—but always with the end firmly and distinctly in view. It involves thinking constantly— not thinking the same thought over and over again, as academics do, but thinking everything afresh every hour. It means thinking in your sleep. It's true: we do think in our sleep. I wake up in the middle of the night and say, '*That's* how we should do this.'"

The complex process of setting up this university—both as a physical plant and as a set of educational programs—has required a certain degree of improvisation. For instance, the administrators have scrambled constantly to obtain enough classroom space. One of the first buildings available—"an old [Kurdish] police building that looked like a Catholic high school, with great, thick walls and tile floors," according to Agresto—was big enough for the university's initial seventy-five students but not for the more than two hundred who registered soon after. "What are we going to do?" Agresto asked at that time. "These kids are going to be sitting on the floors. But the person who took my place—Joshua Mitchell from Georgetown University—said, 'All right. We're going to put up trailers.' So we're educating two hundred or more students in trailers in the parking lot."

Another high-stakes issue concerned how to fund students, many of whom had only the most limited resources to pay for a college education. Agresto explains: "We were taking money out of the general operating funds to cover scholarships. And at that time I had a number of Iraqis who would say, 'We don't want to give you scholarship money. We want to sponsor individual people.' And I said, 'No, no, no. Sponsoring is not a good idea.' By sponsoring they meant, 'We'll pick the students we want you to take, and we want to give the money directly to them. We don't want to give the money to you.'" Agresto found this approach problematic because it might prompt too much intervention by contributors. He goes on to say:

> Basically what they meant was, "We want our workers or our nephews or our nieces or our friends' friends to be accepted as students." And I resisted this. But Josh Mitchell, when he came on, said, "Why are we resisting this, John? Yes, they want to give money to people they know. But we control whether those students get in or not. We've got our standards.

And if people agree to support the students? We have no objection to that. It fosters a sense of connection." I just recently heard that several prominent sponsors are going to give $10 million in sponsorships over the next few years.

In short, agility must be built on a foundation of unity and clarity—especially clarity regarding the standards and values on which you won't compromise. Agility is about turning and adjusting as appropriate while remaining true to the core principles you've established. John Agresto sums up his approach: "It takes absolute clarity and determination as to the end. And a willingness to be insane, chaotic, wild, imaginative, forceful, impetuous, headstrong, and flexible regarding the means."

Agility, it turns out, has a lot in common with perseverance—which isn't how most people think of it. In many of the books and articles on the topic that we've read, agility is described in terms of perceiving changes and obstacles in the environment and reacting quickly. That ability to sense and react is surely a part of agility; for the leaders in our case studies, however, it wasn't the hardest or most crucial part. Changes and obstacles in the environment tend to make their presence known. The real question is: are you flexible and tenacious enough to work with them? Or do you turn your face away, shrug, and think, "Well, that's a change we hadn't foreseen; I guess there's nothing we can do about it now." Do you sit down and give up—or do you find a way to keep moving?

Tata Sky: "So Many Things We Hadn't Planned"

At Tata Sky, leaders showed great agility—and perseverance—in developing and marketing their direct-to-home TV service. As Vikram Kaushik describes:

There were so many things we hadn't actually planned. We always thought that the maximum demand for installation would be over the weekend, not realizing that over the weekend, a lot of people don't want to be bothered. We were taken by surprise when we realized that people wanted the installs done either early in the morning or in the evening on weekdays, because most couples are working and didn't want our engineers coming in when they were not there. So we very quickly had to adapt to that. We very quickly had to ensure that we had people who were available before 8:00 a.m. and would be available after 8:00 at night.

Other problems cropped up that required Tata Sky to adapt and keep moving. "We had constraints because when it's dark, it's difficult to install, especially if they're doing the installation on a terrace where there's no source of light," Kaushik notes. "So we had to quickly adapt to this and see how we could rise to the occasion. There were parts of the country where our installers took a small generator along, to generate the electricity to create the light to do the installation. And consumers were blown away that there was no power, and these guys were still installing because they had this little thing in their van. They just pulled it out and turned it on."

More challenges occurred in the wider competitive landscape. Says Kaushik:

In 2007, the government suddenly announced that they were going to create something called CAS—Conditional Access System for cable—which meant that people would have to buy a set-top box from their cable operator and get digital service in their home. What was interesting about this was that the box wouldn't cost more than a thousand rupees [about US$20], and the cost of each channel would be only five rupees [10 cents]. And you could choose the channel you wanted.

Now, this could have been the death knell for our DTH service, because our cost . . . was 3,000 rupees, and the cost of our subscriptions was much higher than five rupees a channel. But you know what the team did? They said, "Hey, what is the real message?" The real message was that every consumer must have a set-top box in his home in those parts of the four cities where the new service was beginning—Kolkata, Mumbai, Chennai, and Delhi. And they said, "This is an opportunity, not a problem." We could go out and emphasize that it's now mandatory that you must have a set-top box. Given that fact, why would you buy a cheap set-top box from the same old cable operator who you've been frustrated with—when you can buy a world-class DTH service, which *also* supports the box? We were selling 60,000 connections a month. We sold 240,000 in the space of six weeks in those cities.

Everybody was taken aback, because we advertised it. We went to town with it. We hired freelancers who went and knocked on people's doors and said, "We've arrived from Tata Sky. Can we give you a box?" There were road shows as well. The responsiveness in the organization is phenomenal. It was not a small task, because suddenly we needed these extra boxes for those cities. The factories were belting it out. It was quite a remarkable endeavor.

The Strategic Speedometer: Measuring Clarity, Unity, and Agility

The Strategic Speedometer (see figure 2-1) that follows is a quick way to see how your organization or business unit is doing on the people factors of clarity, unity, and agility. Think of it as a way to check the leading indicators of accelerated or decelerated execution and to pinpoint your main trouble spots, or speed bumps.

After combining the results of our Global Speed Survey with our case studies and literature review, we were able to identify nine items—three for each people factor—that correlate most highly with strategic speed. We shared this "speedometer" with a sample of 231 leaders from nearly as many organizations, asking them to complete the assessment with their organization in mind and also to report on the overall speed of their organization. Their responses validated the nine items as predictors of speed and showed that all nine are of roughly equal importance.

The leaders' responses not only validated the items but also revealed these interesting facts:

- To be at par with the faster companies, your overall average score needs to be about 3.75. If your average score is close to 2.75, you are at par with slower companies.

- Even the fastest companies had quite a bit of variation in their ratings of individual items and showed room for improvement on many of the items. Nearly every company, it seems, has an opportunity to increase strategic speed by improving on these people factors.

- Items 1, 2, 6, 7, and 9 received the lowest average ratings from all companies (both the speedy and the not-so-speedy). These items may represent your best opportunities to leapfrog other organizations; if you do well on them, you're likely to stand out.

As you do the assessment you can think about either your entire organization or just the business unit that you lead, be it a function, division, department, or team. *People* means the employees who work in the organization or business unit; *we* means the leaders of the organization or the leaders within your business unit. Once you've completed the Speedometer for yourself, you can read on and learn about some common organizational patterns of high or low clarity, unity, and agility.

FIGURE 2-1

The Strategic Speedometer

Scale:
1 = to a very small extent
5 = to a very large extent
To obtain your overall score, add your ratings and divide by 9: _____.

Clarity

1. People have a shared understanding of our strategy at a detailed level.	1	2	3	4	5
2. People focus their efforts on a critical few priorities.	1	2	3	4	5
3. Our strategy has been translated into concrete and achievable goals and behaviors.	1	2	3	4	5

Unity

4. We have commitment at all levels to the success of our strategy.	1	2	3	4	5
5. We staff strategic initiatives with capable and dedicated team members.	1	2	3	4	5
6. A spirit of teamwork and cross-boundary collaboration is evident throughout the organization.	1	2	3	4	5

Agility

7. People stay open and flexible in the way that goals are met.	1	2	3	4	5
8. People maintain a bias for action while correcting course as needed.	1	2	3	4	5
9. People capture and communicate what they learn from initiatives and projects.	1	2	3	4	5

Patterns of Clarity, Unity, and Agility

It's common for organizations to emphasize just one or two of the people factors and, as a result, to encounter some typical speed bumps. In our practice, four patterns of organizational behavior crop up frequently; we call them *not my problem, everything to everyone,*

myopia utopia, and *boiled frogs*. Each of these patterns is characterized by different levels of clarity, unity, and agility.

Before you read on, look back at your Strategic Speedometer
ratings and determine your own organization's pattern:

- **Clarity:** High, average, or low?

- **Unity:** High, average, or low?

- **Agility:** High, average, or low?

See if you recognize your organization or team in any of the
descriptions below.

Not My Problem: High Clarity,
Low Unity, Average Agility

In this sort of organization, people are clear about what the strategy
is but less clear about how to execute it. The strategy turns into
fragments that each of the many functions or divisions interprets
differently. Noise arises from an emphasis on functional or divi-
sional goals rather than organizational goals. People selectively
execute the strategy in ways that protect their turf. As a result,
silos form and business units work against each other, all in the
name of the corporate strategy. Information tends to stay within
these silos or functions rather than being shared, and in some
cases, information becomes power. Trust erodes, even when people
think they're doing the right thing. Pressure for short-term performance is so high that there is little experimentation or reflection.
The corporate salute is pointing your finger at someone else—it's
not *my* problem, it's *your* problem.

This pattern of behavior can have devastating consequences.
Look at what happened to Enron. Hailed for a decade as a paragon of
speed and innovation by external observers, what was actually going
on inside the firm was a perfect example of "not my problem." Silos
sprang up, turf wars raged, and leaders interpreted the corporate

strategy to suit their personal interests—even when those interests were criminal. In the end, Enron crashed and burned.

Everything to Everyone: Low Clarity, Low Unity, Average-to-High Agility

This type of company has a glorious new strategy. There's only one problem: nobody is doing anything about it. Business goals get plenty of lip service but little focus or accountability.

We're sure you've encountered companies that try to be all things to all people. They jump on every "hot opportunity" they see, but never quite manage to turn any of the opportunities into profitable products or services. They promise their products or services are fast, good, and cheap, when in fact they can deliver on only one or two of those promises; they take this approach because they prize customer satisfaction and don't want to disappoint anyone. Everyone is happy until it's time to deliver and things go wrong. Then, everyone pitches in to make it right: they expedite the order, which disrupts the other orders, and soon everything is being expedited . . . until the company goes out of business—all in the name of customer satisfaction.

This type of organization seems to have a strategy, but it's really just an intention. The intention doesn't help people decide what they should start and stop doing—so they do everything. Some of the dot-com companies of the late 1990s were fine examples of this sort of jumpy, distracted, eager-to-please culture.

Myopia Utopia: Low Clarity, Average-to-High Unity, Low Agility

In this type of organization, there's a heavy reliance on "strong results today" that overlooks the strong behaviors and values necessary for the sustained health of the business—sometimes even for the health of the industry. These organizations are often public companies pushing to maximize shareholder value, and they may encourage "all hands on deck" efforts in order to hit the numbers. In privately held firms, the same approach is sometimes encouraged by pace-setting leaders who believe that speed can be attained if everyone simply works as hard as possible. Pressure for short-term performance is so high that there's little experimentation or reflection and little concern for achieving clarity of direction. There is plenty of camaraderie but little accountability for finding and fixing systemic, long-term problems. Quick and local fixes create a lot of noise in the system. The net result is organizational performance typified by peaks and valleys—potentially very deep valleys from which the firm may never emerge.

Lehman Brothers was an example of a myopia-utopia culture. As Saj-nicole Joni reported in *Harvard Business Review*, "Lehman Brothers had one of the strongest cultures of collaboration on Wall Street, right up until its collapse."[2] Perhaps we should say, instead, that the firm had a culture of *conformity*. On Lehman's management team, dissent wasn't an option, even when the signs of an impending financial crisis began to loom. Conforming, loyal team players were taken care of at Lehman; people who rocked the boat were unappreciated. The utopian bubble, of course, finally burst.

Boiled Frogs: High Clarity, High Unity, Low Agility

How many companies can you name that, after years of success, drop out of the competition—either to fade away or to reemerge after painful restructuring? Think IBM with the PC, Dell computer with the modular assembly process, the entire U.S. automotive business, the music industry, newspapers, and network television. What happens to these companies?

Generally speaking, these sorts of organizations have a very clear strategy and have been able to execute it very well. The seeds of their success, however, also account for their crop failure. They become so focused on what has worked that when things start to go poorly, all they can do is try more of the same, which only exacerbates the situation. It is difficult for such companies to look outside and understand that their business environment has changed—in some cases dramatically. You see this happen all the time with new, nimble competitors. A big player sees a new player entering the market at the low end, so it begins lowering its own prices. It isn't worth it. Soon, the new player begins moving up the chain, learning as it goes. Soon the newcomer is the big player, having put the former big player on its heels.

Like frogs that supposedly won't jump out of a pot when the water is heated very, very slowly—and end up getting boiled to death without ever realizing they are in danger—this type of organization never realizes that it's time to take a leap in a new direction.

Four Leadership Practices That Boost Clarity, Unity, and Agility

We've explored the three people factors and what they look like in action or when they're missing. The next question is *how* do you increase those people factors—both in specific initiatives and in your organization's work overall?

Our case study research revealed that leaders who were successful in driving strategic speed applied four practices consistently. When these practices are strongly present in a company, you can predict with a high degree of certainty that that company is faster and more successful than average. (See appendix A for details.[3]) These four practices comprise:

1. **Affirming strategies:** The first step in driving speed is to ensure all people in the organization know where they're going and are motivated to go there. *An affirmed strategy*

is not only a sound strategy, it's also alive—that is, complete, clear, well communicated, and well understood by all stakeholders. Leaders frequently spend a lot of energy on *formulating* a strategy and expressing it in a statement, but too often the statement exists in a vacuum: incomplete, unexplained, unheeded, and insensitive to context.

2. **Driving initiatives:** *Driving initiatives* is about execution. Without execution, any strategy will slow and eventually die. Senior leaders often assume their job is merely to "sponsor" strategic initiatives. Our research shows that, on the contrary, they must get behind the wheel and drive. Many of the skills that support this leadership practice are project management skills: unfamiliar territory for many executives, but territory they need to master. Though we don't advocate turning senior leaders into project managers, we do know that no initiative is too big to be treated as a project.

3. **Managing climate:** *Climate* is what it feels like to work in a place. Unlike organizational culture, climate is something that leaders have a tremendous amount of control over and that can be managed. Managing climate is a matter of understanding its six dimensions (discussed in chapter 5) and the specific management tactics that improve it. If you can change your organization's climate in positive ways, the resulting changes will boost your employees' motivation, improve their performance, and increase speed.

4. **Cultivating experience:** Like solar, wind, and water power, *experience* is everywhere. Just like that green energy, however, it's rarely captured and put to good use. Most leaders know that smart, skilled, experienced employees are

necessary to the success of an organization and that more experienced employees and teams can move faster than those less experienced. Many leaders, however, don't know how to *cultivate* the experience of their many employees and colleagues—how to capture it, make it visible, refine it, and harness it so that it becomes a powerful driver of results.

Four leadership practices: if you adopt and apply them, strategic speed in your organization or team will increase.

Initiative Execution Versus Everyday Execution

You may have noticed a difference between practices 1 and 2 and practices 3 and 4. The first two—affirming strategies and driving initiatives—come to the fore when there's a need for speed in executing on a *specific initiative or project.* They help reduce the time to value of the initiative and increase the value it contributes to the organization over time. We call this type of execution *initiative execution.*

The latter two practices—managing climate and cultivating experience—come to the fore when there's a need to increase the speed of *the organization's ongoing work.* They help reduce time to value and increase value over time in all the daily tasks and objectives of the individuals and teams you influence. We call this type of execution *everyday execution.*

As a leader, you need both of these lenses on strategic speed. One focuses on rapid execution of discrete strategies, change initiatives, and projects. The other focuses on creating an environment conducive to fast execution of projects and achievement of objectives large and small: an organizational environment that supports speed, every day.

Through these leadership practices managers influence the people factors in a way that drives strategic speed. Each practice affects all three people factors—clarity, unity, and agility—in different ways (see table 2-1).

In chapters 3 through 6, we'll look at each leadership practice in turn and provide techniques for and examples of how to apply it. Each chapter will conclude with a brief self-assessment, so that you can get a sense of how you're doing on that practice.

TABLE 2-1

How the leadership practices boost the people factors

Leadership practice	Increases *clarity* by	Increases *unity* by	Increases *agility* by
Affirming strategies	Ensuring that people understand a strategic direction or intent and their role in supporting it	Emphasizing the importance of each person's buy-in and contributions to executing a strategy or project	Increasing people's awareness of external and internal conditions and their implications for strategic decisions
Driving initiatives	Defining specific objectives, roles, and action plans	Ensuring that everyone knows exactly how their job and behaviors contribute to the success of the whole	Keeping leaders' "hands on the steering wheel" so that course corrections are being made continuously
Managing climate	Giving people opportunities for open dialogue about the organization's goals and objectives	Setting the stage for cross-company collaboration and teamwork	Encouraging ownership, flexibility, and confidence in making decisions and pursuing objectives
Cultivating experience	Allowing people time to formulate and discuss goals and reflect on progress toward meeting them	Expecting each individual to have a perspective, offer insights, and contribute to the learning of the team	Enabling people to learn from experience and apply lessons quickly to emerging problems

THREE

Leaders Affirm Strategies

I N CHAPTER 2, we noted that the first two leadership practices—affirming strategies and driving initiatives—come to the fore when there's a need for speed in *initiative execution*. Although these practices can apply to almost any type of initiative or project, we're going to talk about them here as they apply to large-scale strategic initiatives: big change efforts in which you're trying to implement a new strategy or new direction for your organization or business unit.

In this chapter, we'll focus on affirming strategies. Our Global Speed Survey (see appendix A) confirmed that "Creating a shared understanding of the business strategy" is one of the top leadership capabilities that differentiate faster from slower companies.

Affirming Your Strategy Is the First Step

Strategy affirmation is the first step in initiative execution, because before you can drive speed, you must ensure that your people know where they're going and are motivated to go there. This leadership practice increases *clarity* by ensuring people understand a strategic direction and their role in it; increases *unity* by emphasizing the importance of each person's buy-in and contributions; and increases *agility* by increasing people's awareness of external and internal conditions and their implications for decisions.

An affirmed strategy is not only sound but also complete, clear, and fully endorsed by all those coming on the journey; it serves as a real guide and inspiration to the people who need to execute. Leaders frequently spend a lot of energy on *formulating* a strategy, selecting from among various directions. In the end, they pick one and write it up as a statement, but from the rest of the organization's perspective that statement often does nothing to light the way. It sits in a binder or on a Web site—more like the weak glow from an LCD light than a beacon on a lighthouse.

In many of our case studies we found examples of leaders who didn't just formulate a strategy; they *affirmed* a strategy, and as a result, the strategy became a beacon and an energizer for hundreds or even thousands of people. One such leader is Tom Endersbe of Ameriprise.

Ameriprise: Dream It . . . Do It

Ameriprise Financial is a leading financial planning company located in Minneapolis, Minnesota. Spun off from American Express in 2005, Ameriprise is in the top three hundred of *Fortune* 500 companies and has about half a trillion dollars in invested assets. Ten thousand Ameriprise advisers serve 2.8 million customers—individuals, businesses, and institutions.

In 2007, senior management decided to create better alignment among the company's advisers. The core challenge was that these advisers had different levels of expertise and different levels of tenure within the firm; they achieved different levels of success; and they served a wide variety of clients. Some of them worked directly for

Ameriprise; others were self-employed. Senior management believed that if they could create a higher degree of alignment among the advisers in delivering their value proposition to all their customers, this alignment would help distinguish the firm from its competitors, which would in turn help foster growth. To do so, leaders created an initiative called "Dream It . . . Do It." It was a financial planning model that emphasized the company's desire not just to sell products to customers, but to help customers fulfill their dreams, focusing not just on completing a transaction but on fostering a long-term customer-adviser relationship.

Tom Endersbe, marketing vice president, led the initiative. Endersbe is a seasoned financial adviser and well respected in the financial planning community—in fact, he has been rated as one of the top ten financial planners at Ameriprise. He believed passionately that Ameriprise could differentiate itself from financial brokers who were offering products that increasingly looked like commodities. Rather than compete through products and technology alone, Ameriprise's strategy was to build long-term relationships with customers to enable them to meet their financial needs and to help them make wise decisions on a topic that can be both complex and emotional. The challenge was to get all ten thousand planners on the same page.

To communicate the vision and strategy, Endersbe believed it was critical for leaders at all levels to "get on stage" and speak about the new direction at every opportunity. The Dream It . . . Do It team decided that the best way to foster understanding was to invite all the financial advisers to the company's Minneapolis headquarters to immerse them in the Dream It . . . Do It strategy; doing so would provide opportunities to discuss its purpose and value for them and to give them tools and training to begin applying it with their customers.

The program was a huge success. Turnout was higher than expected (over eight thousand attended), and the advisers said it helped them feel more connected to the company and more in-formed of and committed to the new strategy. The program gave leaders ample opportunities to send a common message and repeat it again and again—not just in one-way broadcasts, but in two-way conversations with small groups and individuals. The message was reinforced through the company's Web site, which provides infor-mation and tools to advisers, and through ongoing webcasts de-signed to help advisers meet their business challenges.

Now that the advisers have a common framework for their role, Endersbe says, they're able to move faster. For example, when he launched a webcast on market volatility that would ordinarily have taken five months to develop, he did it in a few weeks, because the various corporate departments and the advisers cooperated to put it together. "People now know each other's businesses better," he states. "There is a culture of cooperation and speed, a willingness to help; we feel like we're not like everybody else. People feel em-powered to work across the organization."

The good results of Dream It . . . Do It were due largely to the fact that Endersbe and his colleagues didn't merely formulate a strategy; they affirmed it.

When Is a Strategy Not a Strategy?

Even as the business environment has become increasingly com-plex, many strategies have become increasingly simplistic. Some have become so abbreviated that they're little more than catchy phrases. These "strategies" aren't strategies at all—they're just statements of strategic intent, or at best, strategies that are incom-plete. At worst, they're sound bites that provide little guidance for execution. Here are some examples:

- "Our strategy is to be the low-cost provider in our industry."

- "Our strategy is to focus on the customer."

- "Our strategy is to grow through international expansion."

- "Our strategy is to help our clients grow."

A consultant we know once made a presentation to a company's leaders about their strategy. At the same time, he had been working with another company on its own strategic issues. Partway through his presentation, he realized that he was actually describing the other company's strategy to his audience. No one listening to the presentation noticed the mix-up. Both firms' strategy formulations were so vague that, to listeners, they were indistinguishable.

An affirmed strategy is nothing like the business bromides above. It's complete, clear, sensitive to context, communicated well, and fully supported by those who will execute it. While this chapter focuses mostly on the senior leadership team or the team responsible for creating and executing an organization-wide strategy, the lessons are equally important for any team that's accountable for executing a strategy or initiative, whether organization-wide or confined to a particular business unit.

Strategy affirmation consists of three imperatives:

1. **Leaders must understand the components of a complete strategy:** The strategy needs to tell a compelling story in a way that clarifies what you're doing, why you're doing it, and how it will be executed. People must become clear on the organization's direction and how their jobs contribute to success.

2. **The leadership team must be aligned and alert:** By *aligned*, we mean in agreement on the strategy's purpose and components. By *alert*, we mean sensitive to both the external business environment and the organization's internal capabilities. The team needs to be aware of what's going on outside the company and what's possible

inside the company in order to make progress on the strategy.

3. **Leaders must help others buy in to the strategy:** We all know what lack of buy-in looks like: people say they are on board with an initiative or project, but then they fail to show up for meetings, follow through on tasks, or change their behavior in any way—or simply don't give their best efforts. A strategy without real buy-in is one that will never truly get off the ground.

Formulating a strategy is really only a small part of the story. For a strategy to be affirmed, many people—often thousands—must be brought into the process and buy in to the strategy as a result. Strategy affirmation can take longer than many leaders might like, but if it doesn't happen, the entire strategy runs the risk of staying far below the noise-value line forever.

Let's look more closely at each of the three imperatives for affirming strategies.

Understanding the Components of a Strategy

A strategy should be like a great newspaper article. It should grab your attention with a compelling story that draws you in and makes you want to know more. Like a good article, a good strategy leaves you not just clear about its conclusions but also aware of how the writer reached those conclusions and what the implications are for you. It should be clear about what you can and cannot do—about the choices you can make. In addition, it should clarify how and where you will execute those choices. It should finish by providing you with a clear direction for moving forward.

A complete strategy will leave you clear on the *who, what, when, where,* and *how* of the story:

- Who are your customers—and what market segments are they in? Whom do you wish to attract as your employees?

- What is the compelling story that will inspire people to action? What are your differentiators in the marketplace? Will you win in these markets by being the low-cost producer or by being the most innovative? Will you win by providing the best customer service or by having the most reliable products?

- Where will you compete—not just in terms of geography, but also in terms of market segments? Where and how will you create the most value for your markets?

- When will you make strategic moves and in what order? What is the timeline for execution, and what are the milestones? How quickly do you intend to grow the business?

- How will you actually get it done? What are the resources—the core technologies and competencies needed to execute this strategy? To what extent will you achieve your goals organically, though strategic alliances, or through acquisitions? What are the specific points in your strategic plan?

Donald Hambrick and James Fredrickson write about the economic logic of a strategy: how all the pieces fit together in a manner that will generate the economic returns you seek.[1] Southwest Airlines is an example of an organization with great economic logic. Everything this company's leaders have done—from defining who their customers are to selecting the types of planes and routes they will fly—is based on being the low-cost provider of service. Contrast

Southwest with the many less-profitable imitators in the industry who have mimicked some but not all aspects of the low-cost model. Examples have included Ted (United) and Song (Delta). These imitators had legacy systems and processes that were inconsistent with one another or with their strategic intent. While Southwest has been unified around being a low-cost airline, Ted and Song intended to be low-cost but in practice couldn't disengage from all the features and processes that were intertwined with their identity as large service providers. The *who, what, when, where,* and *how* of their strategies didn't hang together and didn't support their marketing taglines; in short, their economic models lacked logic. Southwest has continued to flourish; its competitors have floundered.

Being Aligned and Alert as a Leadership Team

Increasingly, creating and affirming a strategy is a fluid and complex process. Leadership teams have to be more aligned and more alert than ever in response to changes in the external business environment. Business tools such as scenario planning can help, but these tools are only as effective as the leadership teams using them. What are the implications? One of a company's primary goals should be to have a senior leadership team who are aligned in their purposes while remaining alert both to the external environment and to the internal capabilities of the organization.

You'll recall that our Global Speed Survey surfaced ten items that differentiate faster organizations from slower ones (see chapter 1). Three of these items relate directly to leadership teams being "aligned and alert":

- **Senior leaders are closely aligned and committed to the success of initiatives:** This practice also emerged vividly in our case studies; time and again, we heard that the key to the speed of an initiative was that senior leaders had been unanimous and vigorous in their support—and that there had been no turf battles.

- **When making important decisions that affect the company's future, senior leaders usually put forward creative and innovative ideas:** Effective leadership teams are not only sensitive to changes in the business environment, they are also able to devise innovative solutions rather than simply trying harder to do the same old things. These teams are open-minded.

- **Team members are flexible about switching responsibilities to make things easier for one another:** Members of effective strategy teams don't hesitate to assist each other even if doing so isn't part of their official role. They have a genuine appreciation for others' perspectives and situations, and they are willing to help each other out as needed. Underlying this flexibility is a shared understanding of what it is they're creating together.

Why such emphasis on team dynamics in a chapter about strategy? Because an affirmed strategy is always the achievement of a team, not an individual. Even when an individual leader articulates a strategy, it takes a team to pick up that strategy or drop it, bring it to life or let it wither. The quality of the team's thinking (clarity) will determine the quality of the strategy. The degree of team alignment and commitment (unity) will determine the coherence of the strategy and the extent to which anyone does anything with the strategy. And, the extent to which the team is flexible and open to new ways of doing things (agility) will determine whether the strategy is outdated in a month or becomes a living, dynamic guide for the organization.

Being aligned and alert is critical for any team executing a strategic initiative. Think of an initiative or project team that you are leading now: Is there a supportive, safe environment for team members to ask questions? Is it okay for you to say, "I don't know"? Or is it expected that because you're the leader, you should know the answer to every question? Are there formal practices and processes that the team uses to increase the application of learning to work?

At Waypoint LLC, we found a good example of imperatives 1 and 2 of strategy affirmation: a leadership team who have set forth a complete strategy and are both aligned and alert as they execute.

Waypoint: Out of Seven, One

In chapter 2, we shared a brief anecdote about Waypoint, the member-owned organization that brings together seven large regional firms in the food service brokerage industry. Food service brokers represent manufacturers of food- and beverage-related products to schools, restaurants, institutions, distributors, and the like. The industry used to be highly fragmented—historically, there were thousands of brokers, but consolidation began early in the twenty-first century. In 2001 there were forty-five large brokers in the United States; now there are nine. The big regional brokers compete with about one hundred "mom and pop" local brokers. The regional brokers sell about $400 million apiece per year, but it is a low-margin business.

As recounted in chapter 2, seven of the big brokers formed the Waypoint consortium in 2008 to work together to set industry standards, raise the bar on professionalism, and meet customers' needs better. Waypoint represents 80 percent of the geography of the United States and expects to cover 100 percent soon. The brokers are careful about whom they invite to join the organization, as members have to invest effort and money as part of the group. Members agree to abide by majority vote, to meet certain standards, and to be audited. Initiatives have included the one we mentioned in chapter 2, concerning sales force effectiveness, but standardization across the firms goes well beyond the sales process. Waypoint is also prescribing consistent structures, titles, metrics, and other processes.

Among the many keys to speed in this initiative, the elements of strategy affirmation stand out:

- All seven presidents agreed to support the standards and hold one another accountable. There was a high degree of top-down agreement.

- They have agreed to be audited externally on certain specified progress metrics. If a firm doesn't meet the standards, it will be asked to leave the consortium. This agreement fosters even more accountability and incentive to perform.

- The member firms have invited external consultancies to come in and specify best practices. The external groups partner with internal groups, so that the internal people don't struggle to gain credibility and the external consultants don't struggle to understand the internal systems. Credibility and speed come from both groups working hand in hand and overlapping effectively.

In this example we see a senior leadership team (formerly not a team at all, but the heads of seven separate companies) collaborating to adopt an aligned perspective, a detailed blueprint for success, and a willingness to hold one another accountable for sticking to that blueprint. They're also highly aware of the external environment and of their organizations' internal strengths and weaknesses; in fact, this awareness is what drove them to set up the consortium in the first place.

Helping Others Buy In

The third imperative in affirming strategies is helping the rest of the organization or group to buy in.

Gaining people's buy-in begins with how you communicate with them. There are many ways to communicate a strategy to the rest of the organization, and research suggests that the nature of ideal communication isn't what one might think. Paul Nutt, emeritus professor at Fisher College of Business, Ohio State University, has articulated four approaches that leaders can take when it comes to communicating a strategy:

- **Communication by announcements or edicts:** "Here is the strategy, and here's how we're going to execute it."

- **Communication by persuasion:** "All we have to do is sell this to the organization, tell them why it's great, and get them to buy it."

- **Communication by inviting participation:** "Let's involve people in the decision-making process so they'll understand it better and have some stake in the outcome."

- **Communication by intervention:** "Let's create a new understanding of the current situation that creates an awareness of the business case for change."[2]

While companies use all of these communication approaches to greater or lesser degrees, it turns out that the one used least is by far the most effective and the most conducive to speed. That approach is *intervention*. As Nutt says, "Intervention is the best way to implement strategic decisions. When this approach is used, decisions were more apt to be adopted, and the value of the decision was enhanced, in far less time."[3] Intervention essentially builds a case that states: "Here is why what we're doing now isn't good enough." When leaders build such a case, they prompt people to rethink whether the status quo is acceptable, to reexamine what they're doing now, and to imagine ways in which they and the organization might do better. Creating that tension seems to be the best way of igniting change.

Where is the line between intervention and a command-and-control approach to communication? Here's the crux. The command-and-control approach would deliver an edict: "This is what we're going to do, period." With intervention, the goal instead is to create an understanding of the situation that prompts action. To put it another way: command-and-control means, "I'm going to lead my horse to water and then pressure him to drink." (And if you know the adage, you know that this approach is not always successful.) Intervention means, "I'm going to lead my horse to water and create a scenario where he knows he's thirsty, he knows the water will quench his thirst, and he'll drink of his own accord." The key for leaders is describing the situation in a manner that prompts a choice—a choice to take a new road because it so clearly makes sense.

The core of an intervention approach is the collection and systematic presentation of data that indicate the organization's current performance, the performance of comparable companies, and the gap between the two. The comparison companies must be seen as fair comparisons: they must have similar resources and opportunities. The idea is to present clearly your current level of success; to show which of your "neighbors" are attaining greater success; to make it apparent that you too could be achieving that higher level of success; and to let people draw their own conclusions about the pressing need for change. In short, intervention readies the organization for action by making the *reason* for action crystal clear. As a result, people think about the situation differently from how they did before. They take action not just because the boss told them to do it, but because they understand why the actions are desirable.

Nutt's third approach, communication by inviting participation, can also be helpful. "Persuade through involvement" is a maxim that The Forum Corporation has been espousing and teaching for decades, and we know its power. But participation alone, Nutt found, is not terribly effective. Instead, we suggest a hybrid approach: *intervention* combined with *inviting participation*, or "intervene/invite." How should you proceed? First, present the business case for action; then, provide time for people to reflect and inquire about it with senior leaders and with one another, in as many different venues and situations as possible. Once the gap is clearly understood, use task forces to develop plans for closing the gap.

The reason intervene/invite works well is that intervention addresses the rational aspects of motivation, while inviting participation addresses the emotional aspects. If you're skilled at both, you can attend to all sides of getting buy-in.

Holiday Inn: Using the Intervene/Invite Approach

One of the best examples we found of the intervene/invite approach to getting buy-in occurred at Holiday Inn.

Kemmons Wilson founded Holiday Inn in 1952, naming his Memphis, Tennessee, hotel after the title of a popular 1942 movie starring Bing Crosby and Fred Astaire. In 1957, Wilson incorporated the Holiday Inn franchise based on the principles that each property should be standardized, clean, predictable, family-friendly, and readily accessible to road travelers. Innovations such as the Hollidex reservation system and the Hollidome pool design, which turned many hotels into roadside resorts, helped sustain the chain's strong growth. Ten years and one thousand hotels later, Holiday Inn dominated American hotel chains. Wilson's passion for these values helped create a strong branded experience for guests. In the 1980s, though, Holiday Inn had lost market share to competitors, and by the late 1990s, it saw overall service quality diminish in its market category.

In April 2002, Lynne Zappone, vice president of talent development and learning for Holiday Inn, had a conversation with Dan Sweiger, the director of brand management. Sweiger was concerned about falling guest satisfaction scores at many hotels; he told Zappone general managers (GMs) needed a training program in order to improve the scores. Zappone listened carefully, but after a few minutes, looked Sweiger in the eye and told him, "This is more than a one-hit wonder." A low-cost training program just wasn't going to work. With many competitors gaining on Holiday Inn, bolder action was necessary. Zappone slowly won Sweiger over to a much broader approach, but they had no idea if they could get buy-in from Holiday Inn executives or if the program would work— let alone be implemented quickly enough to show results.

They began by building a case for change (*intervention*). With reports on market share, customer satisfaction, and revenue per occupancy, they illustrated to the VP of marketing, and then other executives, why upgrading their guest experience would help bring back the storied Holiday Inn brand. Sweiger and Zappone spent two months gathering support by meeting informally with members of the executive team. They showed them data from hotels that had great customer service, and how those properties consistently outperformed others, despite locations and amenities that were sometimes not as good. The senior management team ultimately gave their approval, along with significantly more resources to meet the challenge of improving the guest experience dramatically.

Even with senior management support, Sweiger and Zappone knew they needed to get buy-in from two other key constituencies: independent owners and general managers (some of whom were also owners). Many owners had been with Holiday Inn for years and were anxious to recapture the preeminence of the brand. Sweiger decided to establish a general manager advisory board to get their thoughts (*inviting participation*).

Zappone was careful to select the right people to join the GM advisory board. With Sweiger and a few others, she developed criteria that would identify some of the GMs who would help them test and develop their ideas around a customer experience initiative (*inviting participation*). One approach they used to recruit the thirty-five advisory board members was to start with a few believers who recognized the need for change. At an annual conference attended by five thousand Holiday Inn hotel managers, a few select GMs made presentations on overhauling their branded guest experience. The head of brand management, Mark Snyder, made a passionate plea: "We're going to have to make some dramatic changes around here to catch our guests' eye, gain their affection, and make them fall in love with us all over again" (*intervention*).

It worked. The passion that was conveyed by the presenters, along with the knowledge that their current approach wasn't delivering the desired results, won many converts.

Thanks to a compelling case for change and multiple conversations soliciting input from different stakeholders, the new Holiday Inn guest experience began to take shape.

Tata Sky: Getting Buy-In

Leaders at Tata Sky worked hard to gain buy-in as they promoted satellite TV services in India. One aspect of this effort was especially effective, but it included a tense experience along the way.

The organization used what leaders called a soft launch in order to test their approach before rolling out the service to their customers throughout the country. That soft launch consisted of all employees receiving a set-top box in their homes. Over the next few months, the company's project management office monitored what was going right and going wrong. CEO Vikram Kaushik describes what happened next:

> We were presenting the whole project to Mr. Ratan Tata
> [chairman of the Tata Group, India's largest conglomerate
> and Tata Sky's owner]. I said that we were also going to do
> a soft launch. And he said, "Can I please have a box to partici-
> pate in the soft launch?" I almost died. Because the soft launch
> is meant to tell you what is *not* working. If you have Mr. Tata
> sitting there and advising you of what was not working—why
> is the box not working? and why is the picture not coming
> through?—that would be curtains. But I said, "Of course,
> Mr. Tata, we'll give you one."

Worried about what could happen, Kaushik postponed sending the box to the chairman. He received a reminder a few weeks later that said: "What happened? I was supposed to get a set-top box." So at the eleventh hour, he sent the box to Tata's home. He sent supervisors to install it and make sure nothing went wrong. Kaushik continues the story:

> He was very happy with the installation. And of course—
> Murphy's Law—within seven days, he got a blue screen in
> the middle of watching something.
>
> He contacted the call center. Once again, there must be
> a god above. The lady who picked up the phone immediately
> understood it was Mr. Tata and brought in her supervisor,
> who then handled the call. All he needed to do was to reboot
> the box. Just switch it off and switch it on again. It was a
> small software thing. It worked like clockwork. At the next
> presentation, he told me, "Your system works. I called the
> call center, and even that worked!"

As a result of the soft launch, approximately two thousand Tata Sky employees had all touched, felt, seen, and experienced how the DTH system worked. They all had the product in their house. This was inviting participation—or persuading through involvement—in the best sense. Kaushik notes: "The soft launch provided a sense of ownership, which is very, very important. These employees were all brand ambassadors, because they were calling their family and friends to see their new system."

Pulling the Pieces Together

We've looked at three imperatives for affirming a strategy: leaders must understand the components of a complete strategy; the leadership team must be aligned and alert; and leaders must help others buy in to the strategy. What does it look like when all three imperatives are put into action, and how do they contribute to strategic speed? Here's a story of a team that did just that, at one of the United States' oldest financial services firms.

Morgan Stanley: Launching a Corporate University

In late 2007, senior management at Morgan Stanley was taking a hard look at the company's learning and development (L&D) function. With fifteen or twenty fragmented departments around the world, L&D was out of sync with CEO John Mack's "one firm" strategy, which emphasized seamless collaboration across business units in service of client needs. As Joanna Crane, former head of global strategy, says: "In every region, there were five different ways of looking at training, at vendors, at what leadership meant. There was just no consistency." Then, in early 2008, the financial crisis brought on by mortgage-backed securities came to a head. Executives within L&D decided to treat the crisis as an opportunity, and they decided to move fast. Their goal was to create and launch a new entity called Morgan Stanley University. Serving all business units and all regions of the firm, MSU would focus on accelerating how leaders learn and make transitions in a rapidly changing landscape.

Outlining the Components of the Strategy. After several weeks of gathering data, the new MSU senior team—made up of some former L&D leaders as well as leaders from other functions—convened for a two-day launch meeting. Using the strategy-canvas technique described in Kim and Mauborgne's *Blue Ocean Strategy*—a process for making leaps in value that lead to competitive advantage—the team collaboratively determined the pillars of a successful strategy for the new corporate university.[4] They challenged themselves to provide value in ways that other L&D groups typically do not, and as a result, several innovative ideas emerged; for example, they realized they might market their strategy consulting, facilitation, and learning expertise in conjunction with line leaders to develop business for the company. The team articulated a three-year strategy to launch and develop MSU in a targeted, phased manner. They were clear on their customers' needs, the sequence of their moves, and their differentiators. They were clear on current capabilities and on what needed to start, stop, and continue. They operationalized each aspect of the strategy, identifying concrete goals, milestones, and necessary resources.

Being Aligned and Alert as a Leadership Team. The outcomes of the launch meeting—absolute clarity about strategy and structure and the shared excitement of becoming a world-class organization in managing talent—were like lightning in a bottle. But while it isn't uncommon for strategy off-sites to result in similar levels of motivation, the momentum is often lost shortly after the people return to their daily work. This senior team, however, maintained high levels of ownership. It was no accident; for in addition to achieving clarity about strategy and structure, the MSU leaders focused on creating the right team environment. One of the rules of engagement from day one was, "Leadership is not allowing others to fail." Making this a team principle had a uniting effect: when things went wrong, leaders within the function helped each other out, sharing resources and information. There were no more clandestine hallway conversations. A wiki was created to enable people to propose changes to tactics for all to review. The respect and trust built in the strategy-mapping process led to levels of openness not previously seen, which in turn helped the team to work through the rough patches, make quick decisions, and run—not walk— through the challenges ahead.

Helping Others Buy in to the Strategy. The MSU team knew that lack of acceptance is the heaviest drag on execution of new strategies. What slows things down isn't that you don't have the right ideas, or the right quality of products and services, or the right technical specifications; what slows things down is people's lack of acceptance of those ideas. The team took as their guide a simple formula: *Quality* × *Acceptance* = *Effectiveness*. If acceptance is zero, it doesn't matter how high the quality is; effectiveness will be zero.

The MSU team continually reached out to stakeholders to articulate the strategy, the reasons for decisions, and their progress. Says Claudine Wolfe, managing director and global head of leadership development and learning technologies, "We engaged other individuals throughout the organization at various levels to get their input and buy-in, so that once we formally executed the strategy, it was almost prewired throughout the organization." The team facilitated executive team meetings, client workshops, and large "town hall" meetings. They partnered closely with the human resources function, which had previously been removed from the L&D groups. CEO John Mack was an early, and critical, proponent. He supported MSU in companywide e-mails and meetings, linking the initiative to goals he thought critical for the firm. In all these interactions, the team emphasized absolutely open and honest communication. Wolfe states the principle thus: "You ask for feedback, and you get it. And you make it safe for people to give you feedback."

The strong focus on affirming the strategy paid off. Whereas similar initiatives that the team members had been involved with in other organizations took anywhere between twenty and twenty-four months to get off the ground, MSU was up and running in four months. Customer satisfaction levels remained high. The team's strategy didn't change during the market upheavals of 2008 and 2009; in fact, it served as an anchor during rough weather. MSU became integrated with the firm's overall strategy and today is seen as having been a key lever in helping the firm to emerge on the other side of the financial crisis stronger than ever.

An Affirmed Strategy—or a Strategy in the Dark?

The first step in achieving strategic speed is having leaders who don't just formulate strategies but also affirm them (see "Affirming Strategies: Reduced Time to Value, Increased Value over Time" for how companies discussed in this chapter achieved results). They know that strategy formulation without strategy affirmation is a recipe for moving slowly or spinning in place.

Think of a strategy that you've created for your organization, division, or team. Is it an affirmed strategy—or a strategy kept in the dark?

Some strategies are like Holiday Inn's strategy to create a new guest experience, or Morgan Stanley's strategy to transform the learning and development function: complete with specifics, articulation,

AFFIRMING STRATEGIES: REDUCED TIME TO VALUE, INCREASED VALUE OVER TIME

Strategic speed isn't merely about going fast. It's about getting above the noise-value line quickly—and staying there. Here's how a few of the organizations featured in this chapter reduced time to value and/or increased value over time.

- Ameriprise took just eighteen months to create consistency in how its ten thousand financial advisers would provide a superior customer experience. Partly as a result, it now enjoys 96 percent adviser retention and has seen a marked increase in customers who select its high-end financial planning capabilities.

- Holiday Inn generated $200 million in incremental revenue within the first year of its customer experience campaign. By the end of the second year, it had doubled its growth in revenue per available room, a common industry metric. The brand enhancements made it one of the top ten brands for customer service in 2008, according to one survey.[a]

- Morgan Stanley University was up and running in four months—one-sixth the time that's typical for strategic initiatives of this sort, and one-third the time that senior management had expected. Later, the consistent, global approach to talent management provided by MSU paved the way for speedy integration in the wake of the firm's merger with Smith Barney.

a. MSN-Zogby Survey, "How Companies Were Rated," *MSN Money*, May 28, 2008.

discussion, communication, and sensitivity to internal and external conditions. A strategy like that is a brilliant beacon; people can see it clearly, see its power, and follow it easily. Others are more like Jim Van Zoren's "strategy" for his IT group at SmartCom: "Work faster and smarter. End of story." A strategy like that keeps everyone in the dark or even worse, like a mirage, leads people astray.

If your strategy is more like Van Zoren's, ask yourself: How can your people move quickly when they're moving in the dark, with only a slogan or two to guide them? And how much faster might they move if you turned on all the lights?

QUICK ASSESSMENT

How Are You Doing on Affirming Strategies?

You can use this quick assessment to size up your personal effectiveness at affirming strategies and identify opportunities for increasing strategic speed.

Scale: 1 = to a very small extent; 5 = to a very great extent

I make sure our strategy addresses the five questions (who, what, when, where, and how).   1   2   3   4   5

I make sure that people are clear on the business case for change.   1   2   3   4   5

I invite discussion of the case for change, in order to build commitment.   1   2   3   4   5

I introduce new strategies in a way that is personal, so people know what's in it for them.   1   2   3   4   5

I hold people accountable for results.   1   2   3   4   5

I work to ensure that the leadership and strategy execution teams I'm part of are aligned and alert.   1   2   3   4   5

I provide opportunities for people to help shape the strategy execution plan.   1   2   3   4   5

To obtain your score on affirming strategies, add your ratings and divide by 7: _____

Interpretation:

- If your score is less than 3.0, you have an opportunity to improve on affirming strategies.

- If your score is between 3.0 and 4.0, you're doing a good job on affirming strategies, but you may see some specific opportunities for improvement.

- If your score is greater than 4.0, you're doing an excellent job on affirming strategies and should share your knowledge and tips with other leaders.

FOUR

Leaders Drive Initiatives

To accelerate initiative execution, senior leaders need to do more than just "sponsor" initiatives; they need to get behind the wheel and drive. Our Global Speed Survey found that one of the key leadership factors differentiating faster companies from slower companies is the presence of "Leaders who can execute strategic projects in a speedy and effective manner." We call this practice *driving initiatives*. Driving initiatives increases *clarity* by defining specific objectives, roles, and plans; increases *unity* by helping each person see exactly how his or her behaviors contribute to the whole; and increases *agility* by keeping leaders' hands "on the steering wheel" so that course corrections can be made.

We agree with the advice offered by Larry Bossidy and Ram Charan: execution shouldn't be left to subordinates while senior leaders stay above the fray and formulate high-level strategy.[1] We find, however, that leaders are seeking more specifics about what execution really means for them. Are they supposed to become micromanagers and sweat every detail? Should they not empower employees? Bossidy and Charan rightly emphasize the value of coaching—but is coaching all that leaders need to do?

In our work with clients, we've found that some leaders aren't clear about how much they need to *drive* strategy execution. Even when leaders do a good job of affirming a strategy, they frequently make the mistake of assuming that their work is done. They announce a strategic shift, tell their employees, "Here's what we're doing and here's why," get a reasonable amount of buy-in, and then . . . they disengage from the process, turning to other matters and waiting for change to happen. This is similar to making a sale and then walking away and not delivering the product or service to the customer. Making the sale is critically important, of course, but it must be followed by doing the work.

Keeping Your Foot on the Accelerator

Chapter 3 was about ensuring that a strategy is complete, clear, and fully endorsed by all who are coming on the journey. That's a critical first step for achieving speed. The next step: identifying *the big things that need to change or be put in place* in the organization to give the strategy traction and ensuring that *those things do indeed change or get put in place*. If leaders fail to do that work, it's as if they took a foot off the accelerator pedal immediately after emerging from the garage; the car naturally, and quickly, comes to a stop.

Other leaders take the opposite approach: they micromanage. Everyone can think of examples of leaders who've slowed the pace of execution to a crawl. It's as if they're constantly tapping the brakes and jerking the steering wheel; again, the car won't go anywhere fast. Most leaders, however, are aware of the dangers of micromanagement and try to avoid it. The more common phenomenon today, and the more typical barrier to speed, is the leader who "wanders off" after strategy affirmation and stops driving.

To see how affirming a strategy and then driving initiatives complement each other, let's look at an example of a couple of leaders who did a good job of both.

Fender: Building the Band

When your customers are the best in their business, you'd better be the best in your business. With customers like Rock and Roll Hall of Fame member Eric Clapton and sixteen-time Grammy Award winner Sting, Fender Musical Instruments Corporation has met this challenge by manufacturing electric guitars, acoustic guitars, and music-related equipment for the past sixty years. In 2006 management stopped to ask themselves, "What about the next twenty years?" The answer was to create a new vision and strategy and several initiatives to drive it. Initial discussions occurred at "the Sedona Meeting," a gathering of leaders in Sedona, Arizona. Says Keith Davis, senior vice president of human resources, "The CEO, the executive team, and some key players went to discuss: What was good about the past? Where are we now? What are we going to become? What do we value? How can we preserve the passion for music that drives us?" This meeting led to the creation of a new company vision ("to champion the spirit of rock-n-roll throughout the world"), mission, values, and goals.

To help the rest of the organization buy in to this new direction, leaders scheduled a two-day meeting for all managers from every segment of the business. Picture a room sprinkled with MBA accountants, professional manufacturing managers, former rock musicians, and amps and sound experts milling around displays of some of the world's best musical instruments. According to Chris Suffolk, vice president of organizational development, the challenge was to get this group to rally around the new vision and, even more important, to create specific goals for their departments. As Suffolk explains, "The senior leaders said, 'Here's our vision, mission, values, and goals for serving music enthusiasts worldwide for the next twenty years.' Then they put the question to the managers, 'How does your department align to these goals?' The managers were thrilled to be part of the process for creating goals linked to the bigger picture for the first time."

Their excitement surprised even Suffolk. As he tells the story, "I arrived at work at seven on Monday morning after the manager meeting. Because of evening gigs, Fender is not especially known for people arriving early. Well, hovering at the door to my office were two senior VPs. I asked, 'Is someone hurt? What's going on?' They said, 'No, we need to share this new spirit and direction with our people. Do you have any more of those pocket cards with the vision, mission, values, and goals?' They were on fire!"

Next came an all-employee meeting to introduce the new direction. The entire corporate office shut down and met at the nearby Scottsdale Center for the Performing Arts. There were bands playing before, during, and after the event. Suffolk says, "Sharing with the employees—now *there's* where the cascade started. What's important around our values? What's important around our vision and mission? What's important around company goals? How will each department align with the others? And we went forward, sharing how employees could be a part of all this and pull the rope in the same direction."

The real payoff, however, came next. Led by Suffolk, a steering committee built a new performance management process that linked individual, department, and company goals together in a clear line of sight to the customer. Every manager took an active role in driving the new performance and professional development, or PPD, process. According to Suffolk, "This wasn't something human resources did *to* the organization, but was instead done *with* the organization—a key factor for success." He emphasizes that "Managers co-led training, with HR, for other managers, and managers led their own department meetings as they explained the process and wrestled with defining and aligning goals. HR provided the training, tools, and support, but the managers really led the implementation."

Suffolk sums up the impact of the new strategy and PPD thus: "While the company has always had goals, the transparency and alignment reached new levels. This was truly an exciting time. Everyone works hard, and everyone wants to know that what they do makes an impact."

To maintain momentum and increase traction with a strategy, leaders must follow up on affirming strategies with these execution steps:

- Identify and structure the specific initiatives that will drive the strategy forward.

- Staff those key initiatives with capable, dedicated teams— not just people who happen to be available.

- Go beyond passive sponsorship to drive those initiatives— actively supporting and coaching the execution team(s), holding them accountable, and assessing and mitigating risks.

Structuring the Specific Initiatives

When an organization is trying to execute a strategy, there needs to be an "initiative hierarchy"—similar to the hierarchy of positions in a traditional organization chart—put in place to make the strategy happen (see figure 4-1).

This hierarchy consists of the strategic initiatives that support the strategy; the projects that make up the strategic initiatives; and the streams of work that make up the projects. If all you have is an

FIGURE 4-1

The initiative hierarchy

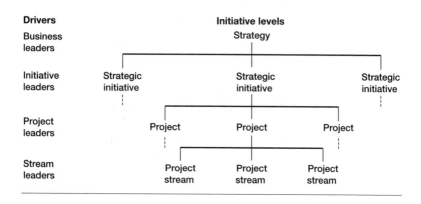

articulated strategy—with no initiatives or projects underneath it to bring it to life and move it forward—then you've got a strategy without legs, so to speak.

Of course the situation is rarely as tidy as this diagram suggests, but the point isn't to have a perfectly neat hierarchy for its own sake. Rather, the point is first to identify the *work* that must happen for a strategy to become reality; and then to *organize* that work into levels in a sensible way, with capable leaders for each level.

The drivers of the work are different at each of the different levels. For the overall strategy or strategic intent, the drivers are business leaders. After that come, in order, the initiative leaders, the project leaders, and the stream leaders. At each level, a leader is responsible for subdividing his or her initiative into logical sub-goals and chunks of work that then become the goals and projects for the next level down.

At Ameriprise, senior leaders created a clear command structure for their initiative. The company appointed one person, Jeff Gans, VP of corporate strategy, to take charge of "Dream It . . . Do It." He reported to senior management and had easy access to them, which provided him with constant direction and support. In addition, he formed several execution teams and assigned them to different tracks, including one for logistics and one for training. Everyone involved knew who was on which team and what their roles and responsibilities were. In short, the initiative hierarchy was clear.

Staffing with Capable Teams

Our research on strategy execution and change management indicates that a critical success factor is *staffing* the execution work with *capable teams*. Senior leaders need to approach strategy execution with the perspective that it is a job—sometimes part-time, sometimes full-time, but a job. Accordingly, you need to (1) hire the right people for the job, (2) equip them to do the job, and (3) give them the time to do the job.

A common mistake is that leaders assume the strategy will simply "become part of everyone's daily work." That is certainly the goal; at some point, you want everyone involved to "cross the river" and be living in the new land. But leaders often forget that it takes work to cross a river, and it takes people whose job it is to make the crossing happen.

It's absolutely essential that the leaders and teams assigned to each strategic initiative and project in the initiative hierarchy are the *right* people—not just the ones who have time on their hands, who sit closest to headquarters, who hold the most senior positions, or who volunteer. They need to be people with the right skills, relationships, and credibility to make happen what needs to happen. Purely expedient choices of team members may get a project off to a quick start, but a lack of clear qualifications and collaborative attitudes will cause the project to remain below the noise-value line—or else climb above it temporarily but then sink rapidly.

We found a positive example of initiative staffing at one of our clients, a large industrial products company. In the course of a multiyear effort to break down the divisions between business segments and functions, a core team of twenty people was formed to drive a key initiative: the creation of an enterprise-wide process that would help unite disparate business units. Although this initiative ended up being a fine example of strategic speed, the process of selecting those twenty people and getting them aligned took several months—and it was time well spent. As one team member put it, "We needed to take the time for people to get on board—or not—with the project. *If you can't change the people, change the people*." He meant that they took time not only to align and train the core team members, but also to assess whether they were the *right* team members. When it turned out that certain people couldn't bring the right level of skill, adaptability, or commitment to the initiative, they were "changed out" in favor of people who could.

In the Morgan Stanley University initiative described in chapter 3, we saw another example of thoughtful, strategic staffing. Many senior leaders of the new corporate university were brought in from outside the existing learning and development departments, thereby creating greater connections to the lines of business. In addition, half the senior team came from outside the United States, in order to support global clients better. Once the new structure for the university was set, every single job description was posted and every previous member of L&D was asked to apply, or reapply, within two weeks for any job at his or her current grade or the grade above. This process exposed some significant talent gaps, but it also allowed some talented people to shine. In terms of time to value, the time it took to "rehire" was easily outweighed by the sheer enthusiasm, effort, and skill that people brought to their new roles.

It's also essential to equip team members to do the job well—by giving them the resources they need—and then to allow them enough time to do the job right. Our research suggests that, on aver-age, you need to ensure that execution teams can spend 50 percent of their time on the work of the team. If that allowance seems unre-alistically high, ask yourself: What will happen if you try to save time by making people do this work around the edges of their exist-ing commitments, and as a result the initiative never gets above the noise-value line? How much noise will be created by people tinker-ing with the initiative in their spare time? Which is preferable: a project that was accomplished in record time because you focused a capable team on it, or a project that never went anywhere be-cause you—and everyone else—treated it as something to be done only as time allowed?

During Tata Sky's efforts to promote direct-to-home satellite TV services in India, CEO Vikram Kaushik made an early decision to structure the company functionally and to place strong emphasis on recruiting true experts for the team. "Given the multiple kinds of activities involved," he explains:

> I recommended to the board that we hire people with functional expertise from companies where they had had similar challenges to manage. We hired people from FedEx to run the supply chain. We hired the sales guy from Colgate-Palmolive in India. Our marketing guy had already sold small cars for Tata [Motors]. The gentleman who came in to manage the subscriber-management systems had run a similar system in Hong Kong and in the Middle East before that. Deepa Watsa [chief HR officer] had worked for several start-up companies, the last one being CapGemini. She worked for Star India before joining Tata Sky, so she had an idea of the broadcast industry as well. The chief technology officer had set up the uplink facility for Star.

The reasons for this approach were twofold. First, precisely be-cause these people possessed expertise in their respective fields,

Kaushik expected them to handle successfully a project that would ramp up very quickly. Second, these people would be able to innovate and adapt—and to help their direct reports innovate and adapt—to the requirements of the new business. The decision to staff the start-up this way "was a hunch," says Kaushik, "but it turned out to be right."

He goes on to state: "Apart from the fact that this team of people had the expertise, the second decision we took was complete empowerment. Once you hire an expert, you don't get in his or her way. This was a very important component of the way we started the company."

Driving the Initiative

The final step is to drive the initiative actively rather than merely being a "sponsor." In short, leaders must get involved and stay involved. Because this step is often complex, we've devised what we call the Execution Model—a research-based approach to ensuring the success of a strategic initiative.

This model is the result of an intensive research project that looked at the factors that predict successful strategy execution. As we mentioned at the start of chapter 1, only 30 percent of strategic initiatives fully succeed on time. And for those strategic initiatives that are partially successful, the average gap between the strategy's potential and actual performance represents a 37 percent decrease in results.[2] Our research identified seven success factors that leaders must manage in order to increase the chances that their strategy or initiative will be among the successful 30 percent. The factors are: *team capability*, *course correction*, *behavior change*, *work effort*, *change magnitude*, *leadership involvement*, and *employee support*. Together, these seven factors are predictive of execution success or failure. For each factor, the Execution Model provides a guiding principle and a set of key strategies designed to enhance execution success and mitigate vulnerabilities (see table 4-1).

Not surprisingly, these seven execution success factors are just a little about processes and technology and a whole lot about *people*. Here's a brief description of each factor and what is involved in applying it.

1. **Team capability:** The degree to which a team and its leader are capable of successful execution.

   Key strategies: As noted above, this factor is one of the strongest predictors of the success of a strategic initiative. It means you should assemble a team from the most effective members, not just the "usual suspects." In hiring or assigning team members, identify the ideal team member profile in advance, and then recruit for it. Do everything possible to inspire (and require) team members to work together cohesively and effectively. Provide adequate resources to the team during their

TABLE 4-1

The execution model

Success factor	Guiding principle
1. Team capability	Deploy strong execution teams
2. Course correction	Create a robust coordination system
3. Behavior change	Make the changes clear and real
4. Work effort	Acknowledge and manage workload pressure
5. Change magnitude	Keep things simple and consistent
6. Leadership involvement	Spotlight leadership visibility and consensus
7. Employee support	Cultivate manager and frontline participation

work. Create clear expectations in advance for team member performance. Make sure the team members can dedicate ample time to the initiative.

2. **Course correction:** The efficacy with which the team collects and reviews information about the initiative and makes course corrections to enhance strategy execution.

   Key strategies: For starters, establish effective measures of progress and success. Create control systems to assess progress, and take into account the reactions and concerns of stakeholders. Then, conduct regular, meaningful progress reviews. Empower the team to make needed adjustments.

3. **Behavior change:** The degree to which people must change their behaviors in order for the initiative to succeed.

   Key strategies: To focus on this factor, identify the type of behavior changes required by new strategies, processes, technologies, and methods. The greater the degree of behavior change required by the new strategy, the more you need to help people understand and deal with those changes. Define a clear, unambiguous image of the future state and how people are acting in it. Both early on and throughout the initiative, provide plenty of training and support.

4. **Work effort:** The amount of additional work people must do in order to implement the strategy.

   Key strategies: You need to develop a realistic picture of people's existing and projected workloads that the initiative may increase. This may mean phasing in new work gradually. It's critical to communicate accurately and honestly about the effort required. In addition, try to make changes that reduce complexity in people's work instead of increasing it.

5. **Change magnitude:** Both the extent of the organization affected by the strategy and the strategy's consistency with the existing culture.

   Key strategies: Be practical about the magnitude of change that the organization can handle. Ideally, introduce changes in stages, in order to manage the impact on people in the organization. Create management processes that reduce rather than add complexity. Be thoughtful and intentional about making changes to culture and values.

6. **Leadership involvement:** The degree to which top leadership and senior sponsors are visibly, actively, and continuously involved in and supportive of the initiative.

   Key strategies: Engage and maintain the involvement and commitment of senior leaders for the duration of the initiative. Orchestrate ways for them to assume visible responsibility for it. Engage senior leaders in providing consistent, unified, and effective communication, and make sure they know what resources are required to make the initiative a success.

7. **Employee support:** The degree to which the people most affected by the change—for example, managers and frontline employees—visibly and actively support the initiative.

   Key strategies: Clearly articulate the purpose and importance of the strategic initiative in plain terms. Create meaning by connecting personally with people, exploring their concerns and ideas, and being sensitive to the anxiety they may feel about changes in their jobs. Ask for people's input, and show that their input has impact. Throughout, maintain a focus on outcomes, and reward commitment.

Note that these seven factors can and should be applied by leaders at all levels of the initiative hierarchy. Sometimes people think that, for example, a business leader doesn't have to think about behavior change, or a project stream leader doesn't have to think about change magnitude. This is not the case. Leaders may adjust these factors to suit their level, but the same factors apply from top to bottom of the hierarchy.

We use the Execution Model, in the form of an assessment, to help leadership teams diagnose where their execution efforts are strong and where they may need help. Since scores on the seven factors predict success (or failure), it's a good idea to assess your initiatives frequently using this model, so that you can pinpoint the spots where you're vulnerable and take steps to mitigate risk.

The Centrality of Behavior Change

Of all the execution success factors above, behavior change (success factor 3) is the one that leaders tend to overlook or misunderstand most often. Lack of attention to this success factor is a huge barrier to speed in many of the firms that we've assisted. If you think back to Jim Van Zoren at SmartCom, you'll recall that he was big on exhorting his team to move faster but not so big on specifying what, exactly, they needed to be doing differently in their daily work. When he outsourced the billing systems to Worldwide Technology, his bold vision caught the attention of the press, but he apparently never translated the vision into the practical, specific changes that would need to take hold in people's jobs and behaviors in order to facilitate communication between teams on opposite sides of the world.

Senior leaders sometimes think behavior change is not what they should be worrying about. They assume that it's "HR's job" or "the frontline managers' job" to coach their employees in specific behaviors that will bring the strategy to life. While skills training may indeed fall under HR's purview, and while daily coaching may indeed be the job of the frontline manager, it is nevertheless up to senior leaders to foster the following changes:

- Articulate a vision that includes some *specifics* on what people in key roles up and down the organization need to be *doing differently.*

- Put a process in place that gets everyone in the organization *thinking and planning* about what the strategy means for *them* in their daily work.

- Insist that managers *hold people accountable for* those behavior changes.

These are not activities that can be left to chance or delegated entirely to HR. In fact, the organization's top team needs to be the one making sure these changes occur.

LaFayette: Giving Touchstones More Weight

Here's an example (in which the names and the industry have been changed) of a company that gave traction to its strategy by ensuring that employees up and down the firm knew what the strategy meant for them and their daily work. For many years, leaders in the Australian division of LaFayette, a global consumer products company, have specified what they call their "touchstones." According to Lara Russell, learning and development manager, the touchstones are "the main drivers to get us to where we want to go." These key themes are presented within the company each year. "This year we've chosen customer focus, brand performance, people, and culture," Russell says. "We'll probably roll those over into the coming years as well, because I think they really are the foundations of our strategy."

But the touchstone concept, though good in theory, was problematic in practice. As Russell explains:

> The year the touchstone initiative began, it was basically run by members of the leadership team. We had town hall meetings where everybody got together and the concept was introduced. But unless you were actually on a touchstone team working on a particular project, you basically checked out of the idea; it became, "Yeah, that's great. That's happening over there, but it has nothing to do with me." For the leadership team, that wasn't acceptable, because the touchstones are what we consider to be the pillars of our business. When you've only got 10 percent of your business actually checked into that idea, that's problematic.

These challenges required leaders at LaFayette to put a more thorough execution plan in place. Says Russell, "This time around, we still did what we call the Touchstone Day. We gathered people from throughout the business, the same as we had the year before. We got them to brainstorm what they felt was important to work on for the coming year. But what we did differently was that we worked on a strategy map as the leadership team. We then cascaded that down through the firm so that every department worked on a departmental planning tool." This planning tool spelled out the key things that people in specific roles needed to be doing differently in specific situations. For example, what did "customer focus" really look like for each department? What were the essential behaviors that would demonstrate customer focus? The tool also spelled out the organizational enablers—skills, processes, policies, metrics, manager actions, and so on—that would support those behavior changes. The departmental planning tools became the specific roadmaps for each work group and each individual—roadmaps that allowed them not only to see the touchstones clearly, but to bring them to life.

"So today," says Russell, "the four touchstones show up in the objectives of every single person within our business."

One of the key points of this chapter—and precisely what leaders often don't understand—is that the broad strategic statements issued by management teams are seldom translated down to what they mean for the work of individual employees, who are left wondering, "What does this strategy statement have to do with my job?" It seems obvious, but if you want anything to happen in an organization—if you want to implement a strategy—it has to take hold in people's work, behaviors, and attitudes.

Wolters Kluwer Financial Services: Driving Customer Focus

Here's the story of a leader at the middle level of an organization who executed a customer-focused strategy within his business unit, using all the driving initiatives steps we've discussed.

Darin Byrne is senior director of professional services at Wolters Kluwer Financial Services, a customer unit of Wolters Kluwer, a global information services company. This unit serves banking, mortgage, securities, insurance, and indirect lending institutions—selling software, documents, analytical tools, and training and consulting services to help its customers manage regulatory compliance and operational risk.

In a recent initiative, Byrne and his colleagues worked to make their company's professional services department a profit center and a growth driver for the firm. Branded internally as "Consultative Service," the initiative provides the company's service professionals with the tools and techniques to act as value-added, strategic providers to their customers.

Byrne's involvement in this initiative went far beyond the planning phases. "For me personally," he says, "it came down to a conviction that this is how the organization should behave. It was fundamental—not something we could really wait on. Knowing I had the mandate to make this organization profitable and keep it growing, I needed to develop people who have a consistent understanding of how to be consultative in a relationship with customers." But fostering the initiative required more than just setting the wheels in motion. Byrne goes on to say: "We couldn't just rely on our best people's practices to rub off on others in the organization. We needed to draw out the concept that service doesn't just stop when the product is delivered or when the order is fulfilled."

Obtaining an effective response from employees involved in the initiative required ongoing energy and participation from Byrne. "Once we started the pilot," he explains, "I reiterated at each quarterly departmental meeting where we were with the rollout, why it was important to our mission, and what our objectives were. When we did the first training session, I attended it." And, after his initial involvement, Byrne made a commitment to interacting regularly with the participants—both to emphasize its importance and to take part in moving the process forward: "Every time we redelivered the training, I went in at the beginning and commented on why we're doing it. At the close of the training, I went back and asked people what they learned, how it could be applied, and what they considered to be the important concepts. I also told stories—for example, a story about an associate in our organization who used the principles to turn a negative interaction with a customer into a positive situation that resulted in the additional referral of thousands of dollars in sales."

The pilot program at Wolters Kluwer Financial Services is regarded as highly successful within the company, and a larger version of the initiative is forthcoming. Byrne's conclusions: "Personal involvement is crucial. When you talk about strategic speed and leadership, you can't just delegate. The leader has to be visibly supportive, visibly involved, and committing his or her own time and effort to drive it."

Driving Initiatives: Merely Project Management?

Does all this talk about driving initiatives sound a bit like "plain old project management"? If you think so, you're right. Truth be told, this question comes up a lot when we discuss these issues with our clients. They'll say, "Well, you're just talking about project management"—and what they mean is, everyone knows that project management is important, but project management is something that project managers do, not something that senior leaders do.

We beg to differ. We are indeed talking about project management, and we believe it is part of every leader's job One of the insights leaders tend to reach when we work closely with them on execution is, "Aha!—we need to treat *this* [the strategy or initiative they're working on] like a project." Project management, it turns out, is critical to strategic speed. We haven't yet encountered an initiative that is too big to be treated like a project. If you want to execute speedily on a new strategy, treat it like a project. If you want to increase the overall speed of your organization, teach project management skills and insist on project management disciplines.

Here's what we suggest: if it's difficult to think of your job as project management, or if that term doesn't feel right, call it *execution management*. We don't expect senior leaders to spend their days managing small projects, but we know that execution is a CEO's job just as much as it is a middle manager's job. We'll conclude this chapter with a story of one CEO who thinks of execution as very much his job.

Informa: Execution at the Top

Peter Rigby is the CEO of Informa, a U.K.-based company that provides publishing, conferences, and performance improvement services. Its publishing roots go back to 1734, when *Lloyd's List*, the world's oldest continuously published journal, began to report on shipping news. In 2005, Rigby and his leadership team made a deal to acquire IIR, another media company, in record time: just five days elapsed between when the opportunity was presented and when the deal was signed.

More important from our perspective, though, was that Rigby and his team sped up the process of making the deal *work*—that is, ensuring that the combined company achieved value quickly. They created a ninety-day integration plan that addressed issues from technology systems to marketing to consolidation of businesses. The implementation team was made up of senior people who all knew their particular businesses well. Individual business leaders were given authority to conduct their own due diligence and run their part of the plan. "We had all the data and knew the constraints," says Rigby. "We had lots of checklists." And the team made people issues a huge part of the plan. Rigby made a point of building strong relationships with all the IIR business unit heads; in the first thirty days, he visited every new office worldwide to reassure people that jobs would be retained, to convey the firm's vision, to convey the benefits of the acquisition to them, and to persuade them to stay on board.

Thanks to his diligent execution and follow-through, Rigby ended up with that relatively rare thing: an acquisition that creates value. Not only was there no decline in performance across Informa as a result of the substantial organizational changes, but the former IIR units grew significantly over the next four years.

Driving initiatives is sound practice for all leaders—from CEOs, to midlevel managers, to team leaders, to project managers. (See "Driving Initiatives: Reduced Time to Value, Increased Value over Time" for how companies discussed in this chapter achieved results.) Leaders at all levels can increase the speed of their initiatives by following these points of advice:

- Take the discipline of project management (or execution management) seriously.

- Follow the execution steps: identify and structure initiatives; staff the initiatives with capable teams; and go beyond mere sponsorship to *drive* initiatives.

- Articulate a vision that includes the specific ways in which people need to think and behave differently in order for the strategy to take hold.

DRIVING INITIATIVES: REDUCED TIME TO VALUE, INCREASED VALUE OVER TIME

- Tata Sky achieved its goal of reaching one million connections by the end of its first year of operation. It then took only another ten months to reach two million connections and just seven more months to reach three million. By 2009 the company had a retail network that covered more than seven thousand towns in India, with four million subscribers.

- The Wolters Kluwer consultative service initiative yielded nearly 650 leads in the first three quarters of 2009 valued at over $112,000 in potential sales, including $45,000 in closed sales. Revenue for the group was 15.8 percent ahead of budget.

- Informa completed the IIR acquisition deal in five days and fully integrated the IIR companies within ninety days. Since the merger, the former IIR units have grown at a rate of more than 10 percent per year, have reduced their cost structures, and have met the target for return on capital invested.

Leaders who take the above steps will find that not only do people in their organization have a clear view of the destination; they are also striding confidently down the road.

QUICK ASSESSMENT

How Are You Doing on Driving Initiatives?

You can use this quick assessment to size up your personal effectiveness at driving initiatives and identify opportunities for increasing strategic speed.

Scale: 1 = to a very small extent; 5 = to a very great extent

I stay involved in driving initiatives forward, rather than announcing them and moving on.   1   2   3   4   5

I communicate a vivid picture of the specific changes people need to make.   1   2   3   4   5

I treat strategic initiatives like projects, with leaders, teams, goals, budgets, and so on.   1   2   3   4   5

I ensure that execution teams can devote at least 50 percent of their time to the initiative.   1   2   3   4   5

I identify and remove impediments to people making needed behavior changes.   1   2   3   4   5

I involve the entire execution team in creating the plan, rather than doing it myself.   1   2   3   4   5

I use the same care in selecting team members for an initiative that I would in hiring a new employee.   1   2   3   4   5

To obtain your score on driving initiatives, add your ratings and divide by 7: _____

Interpretation:

- If your score is less than 3.0, you have an opportunity to improve on driving initiatives.

- If your score is between 3.0 and 4.0, you're doing a good job on driving initiatives, but you may see some specific opportunities for improvement.

- If your score is greater than 4.0, you're doing an excellent job on driving initiatives and should share your knowledge and tips with other leaders.

FIVE

Leaders Manage Climate

W E NOW SHIFT OUR ATTENTION to two leadership practices that help increase speed not only when you're dealing
with a specific strategic initiative or large project, but also when
you want to increase the speed of an organization's or team's daily
work. Managing climate is the first of these drivers of "everyday execution." Managing climate increases *clarity* by giving people opportunities for dialogue about goals and objectives; increases *unity*
by setting the stage for collaboration and teamwork; and increases
agility by encouraging flexibility and confidence in making decisions and pursuing goals.

Simply put, climate is people's perceptions of the work
environment—what it feels like to work in a place. (A more technical definition of climate is "a set of measurable properties of the
work environment, based on the collective perceptions of the people who live and work in the environment and demonstrated to influence their motivation and behavior."[1]) According to Forum's Global
Speed Survey, another of the leadership factors differentiating

faster companies from slower companies is "Leaders who create a positive climate."

George Litwin and Robert Stringer of Harvard Business School first developed the concept of organizational climate in 1968. They demonstrated that certain leadership styles produce a positive organizational climate that in turn has an impact on motivation and performance.[2] By 1974, Litwin, working with The Forum Corporation, was already using an Organizational Climate and Practices Questionnaire to improve leadership, climate, and performance in organizations across industries.[3] Since then, many studies done at Forum and elsewhere have shown that companies can improve their performance and accelerate execution dramatically by managing climate.[4]

Facts About Climate

Sometimes people assume that climate is unchangeable—"just the way things are." Or else they assume that if a workplace has a "good" climate, it simply means that the workplace is fun and relaxing. But climate is more important and more powerful than that. Says one researcher: "A positive work climate is not a fun-filled place, a lot of warm fuzzy stuff, or a place for relaxation; it is . . . conducive to creative, productive work."[5]

People also sometimes think that climate is the same as culture. It isn't. Although the terms are often used interchangeably, they have very different meanings. An organization's culture is rooted in the values and assumptions that the organization's founders embed in it from the beginning. Culture is one of the ways in which an organization preserves its identity and distinguishes itself from others. Conservative by nature, culture is slow-moving and hard to change. Climate, in contrast, is a more immediate and fluid phenomenon. Because climate is more malleable, it can be changed in weeks or even days.

What makes climate so powerful is that it is both *manageable* and *linked to performance*. Managers can change climate fairly easily, and the resulting changes influence how motivated people feel and how well they perform. But perhaps the best news about climate is that it's a relatively low-cost way to achieve big improvements in organizational performance—and to do so quickly. That's because a shift in climate requires no large investment in technology, no complex acquisitions, no redoing of strategy, no decisions to enter new markets. To shift climate, all you need to do is get leaders throughout your organization to take some fairly simple actions. Granted, getting leaders to change their behavior isn't a piece of cake, but consider which is preferable: spending $20 million on a high-end performance management system, performance support technologies, and process reengineering for your entire company; or spending $500,000 to help all your leaders know how to create a positive, productive climate that's conducive to speed? Climate is a true organizational *lever*: give it a small push, and it will move mountains.

Why Climate Matters

Climate has been shown to influence business results. Consider this evidence:

- A study by Daniel Goleman found that climate accounted for 33 percent of the difference among company business units in their financial performance.[6] For example, a leading insurance company found that 71 percent of its work units with the best climate had above-average sales results, while only 18 percent of those with the worst climate had above-average results.

- A recent study of ninety-six of the world's leading sales organizations discovered that high scores on the climate dimensions of clarity, commitment, responsibility, and recognition were predictive of high overall performance.[7]

- A luxury hotel implemented leadership training and coaching that resulted in a 20 percent improvement in organizational climate. The climate improvement correlated with a 19.6 percent drop in employee turnover, a 23 percent increase in market share, and an 8.2 percent improvement in guest satisfaction scores.[8]

Another benefit of a positive climate is that your *customers* feel it, and it affects how much they want to do business with you. Consider these facts:

- A group of media companies experienced 87 percent buyer retention for those business units with a highly positive climate, versus 54 percent buyer retention for units with a negative climate.[9]

- At a large financial services organization, 41 percent of the customers of units with a highly positive climate increased their level of business with these units over 2.5 years, while only 18 percent of the customers of units with a negative climate increased their level of business.[10]

Climate is a critical part not just of the employee experience, but of the customer experience as well. Customers tend to sense climate quite quickly—often in the course of a fifteen-minute visit to a shop, organization, or work group. And their perceptions of climate match employee perceptions closely.[11] The climate that customers perceive makes a strong impact on their experience, their satisfaction, and their desire to work with you.

For a more immediate example of why climate matters, think back to the SmartCom example in the prologue. The poor climate

Van Zoren inadvertently created in his IT group contributed not only to demoralized, hostile employees, but also to chronically missed deadlines, mistrustful internal customers, and the loss of a huge customer contract.

How Climate Works

Perhaps you've worked in a job where a new manager came in with a very different style than his or her predecessor. Perhaps the new manager asked for your ideas and opinions, while the previous one had a command-and-control style. Or perhaps the new manager was vague and vacillating about expectations, while the previous one had been crystal clear. How quickly did the climate change? How did it affect your unit's performance? Many people can offer dramatic vignettes of such situations—morale rising or slumping, employees feeling empowered or debilitated, productivity increasing or diminishing. Why such quick, clear responses? Simply because, unlike culture, climate is influenced rapidly and directly by the behavior of employees' immediate managers.

Figure 5-1 shows how climate works. While things like the external environment and the strategy set by top management do influence climate, the actions taken by direct managers have by far the greatest effect. (In fact, our research on climate indicates that 70 percent of the variance in climate between work units is attributable to what the direct managers of those work units do.) Climate, in turn, drives individual motivation, which drives individual speed of execution, which drives organizational speed of execution and overall performance.

Tata Sky: A Positive Climate Enhances Speed

Once again, Tata Sky provides a striking example: in this case, of how positive climate builds confidence and motivation, which in turn help increase speed. Chief HR officer Deepa Watsa notes how

FIGURE 5-1

FIGURE 5-1

How climate works

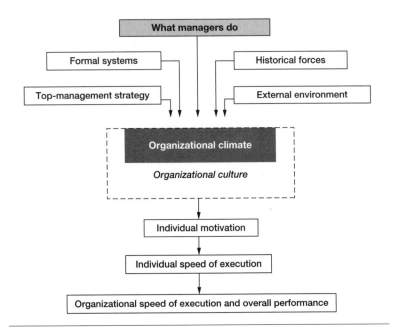

CEO Vikram Kaushik powerfully affected the company's climate: "Vikram's complete belief that we could do it put all of us on a real high. And of course there was the sense of commitment that each one of us had. We were absolutely committed to making this happen on time, because we wanted to live up to his expectations and his belief—the faith that he had in all of us."

Kaushik himself explains the source of his confidence and energy: "I got it from the shareholders. Because I must say that both Tata and Newscorp [News Corporation, Star's parent company] really let us do our thing. They said, 'The money is available, now do it your way.' Of course, we had to go back to the board every month and explain what we were doing, which was fine. In turn I could then pass confidence and energy down, and it was working . . . [We all] had no issues about getting our hands dirty. None of us minded doing anything. Everybody chipped in. Everybody carried their weight."

Watsa also describes how she and her team decided to launch an assessment of their organizational climate so they could determine how to improve it. This initiative, she says, required a leap of faith.

> My first question was, "Is this the right time? There's a world economic crisis. Everything is falling apart around us. We don't know what's going to happen to currency. We don't know what's going to happen to interest rates. Is this the right time to get involved in this other evaluation of our corporate culture? Is it going to cost money? This is a very unsettling time. People are concerned about their jobs. Not to mention that there are five competitors in the fray." And I asked these questions of the executive team during one Monday morning meeting when we do our national video-conference. They all said, "Yes, we should do it."

CEO Kaushik has additional thoughts on climate and its power to foster strategic speed: "I think what matters is the sense of personal responsibility, the sense of involvement, the importance given to motivation, the importance given to a pretty rigorous appraisal system in the company," he states. "We've been very generous with people . . . And yet everybody knows if they don't perform, then they don't get the rewards. So we've tried to make sure that we don't lose track of the really hard-nosed professional measurements, which are necessary to run an effective company. But equally, the face of our normal day-to-day interactions is very open and very relaxed. We don't create unnecessary hysteria or insecurities. There is a school of thought that people must be made insecure for them to perform well. I've never believed in it."

The Dimensions of Climate

Our research over four decades reveals six climate dimensions:

1. Clarity

2. Standards

3. Commitment

4. Responsibility

5. Recognition

6. Teamwork

By understanding these dimensions and how they can combine and interact to affect climate, you can take an important step toward accelerating everyday execution in your team. Notice that each dimension is defined in terms of how people *perceive* the work environment—what it feels like to work in that place (see table 5-1).

Clarity

The first climate dimension, clarity, is the degree to which employees understand the organization's goals and policies and the requirements of their jobs. (We also used the word *clarity* for one of the three people factors described in chapter 2. *Clarity* as a people factor means lucidity, awareness, perspicacity, or understanding. Like agility and unity, it's a quality that people *have* or *are*: "People *are clear* on where we are going." *Clarity* as a climate dimension means structure, order, or directedness. It is an aspect of how the workplace *feels*— structured, ordered, well-directed: "Things around here *feel clear.*" But for leaders, it really comes to the same thing: you want to be sure that people are clear and that things feel clear to them.)

TABLE 5-1

Climate dimensions

Dimension	Definition
Clarity	The degree to which people understand the organization's goals and policies and the extent to which they understand the requirements of their jobs
Standards	The emphasis people feel that management puts on high standards of performance, and the degree to which pressure is exerted to improve performance
Commitment	The degree to which people are dedicated to achieving goals and contributing to the organization's success
Responsibility	The extent to which people feel personally responsible for their work and accountable for solving problems and making decisions
Teamwork	The degree to which people feel they belong to an organization characterized by cohesion, mutual support, trust, and pride
Recognition	The degree to which people feel that they are rewarded and recognized for doing good work, and that rewards are clearly related to performance excellence

An excellent example of the clarity dimension occurred at Abbott Vascular in China. This company offers a comprehensive portfolio of vessel closure, endovascular, and coronary products that are recognized for their safety, effectiveness, and ease of use in treating patients with vascular disease. Harvinder Singh was appointed in 2006 as regional director and general manager of commercial operations for greater China. His strategy was to expand the Abbott Vascular footprint in China and create a market-leading vascular business. Abbott had recently acquired a company in China, and Singh's mission was to facilitate the post-acquisition integration and improve the performance of the China business.

When Singh took the reins, he faced a formidable challenge: revenue had declined significantly from the previous year, and employee turnover was alarmingly high. Most of the senior managers had left in the past six months. Surveys found that only 50 percent of employees believed that Abbott could succeed in the China market. Singh knew he needed to act quickly to restore confidence and improve climate. He focused first on setting a clear goal of achieving a strong presence and ultimately market leadership in China (rather than simply copying competitors), and then communicating that direction to the team. Singh and his leadership team met regularly with employees to let them know that he was there to rebuild the company, that they would succeed, and that he needed their help. He repeated the message at every opportunity. The next level of leadership followed through by continuing to communicate the message and encourage employees to believe in and sell the Abbott brand. In addition, the leadership team spent lots of time with middle managers who had been skeptical, explaining exactly what the plans were for the business and how they could contribute.

By constantly keeping employees informed about the direction and the progress they were making, Singh created a climate of high clarity. As a result, revenue at the company went from a year-over-year decrease of 25 percent to an increase of more than 75 percent, and employee turnover decreased from 45 percent to 6 percent. Singh says, "Driving this change was like pushing a big rock. Initially it was tough to get everyone to align and push in one direction. Once the rock started moving, though, people saw the momentum building, and they got excited and pushed harder."

Standards

The second dimension of climate is the emphasis that management places on high performance standards and the amount of pressure that leaders exert on teams to improve their performance. As

Vikram Kaushik of Tata Sky noted, a positive climate doesn't mean a completely relaxed one. High, clear standards for performance are motivating to leaders and employees alike.

We saw in chapter 2 how standards were important to John Agresto, cofounder and current board member of the American University of Iraq. Agresto and his colleagues established and organized a prestigious academic institution in Kurdistan over the course of just a few years. One crucial, early decision concerned the admissions standards for students. We described how Agresto held to admissions standards and yet demonstrated agility in how sponsors could support students who gained admission. Another aspect of this example, however, is the way in which those high standards affected the climate of the institution.

Describing a small graduate-level MBA program, Agresto states, "No one can enter without an English language facility of at least what's known as TOEFL 550"—a fairly high score on the test of English as a foreign language. This score would establish standards for facility in the language used throughout the university. Agresto notes, however, that in post-Saddam Iraq, "Money talks. You can get whatever you want by paying. Well, we wanted to make a reputation by saying, *standards* talk." In short, Agresto and his cofounders wanted to create a climate in which academic excellence and intellectual rigor could flourish.

But establishing standards led to some controversy. At one point, a benefactor of the new university wanted his niece to be accepted into the program. Unfortunately, her TOEFL score was below the acceptable minimum. "We said, 'Absolutely not. We can't take her,'" Agresto explains. "And he couldn't believe it." Tensions ensued. Agresto held his ground. The result was an important underscoring of the university's standards. He elaborates: "The students soon got wind of this situation—that we would turn down a major donor's relative. This allowed the students to realize that people can't buy their way in; it doesn't matter who your uncle is, who your father is, or how much money they have. Now students could brag that each and every one of them got in on merit alone. You can imagine how wonderfully this set us apart in Iraq." The resulting high standards have helped to foster a climate of high academic performance at this new university.

Commitment

Commitment is the degree to which people are dedicated to achieving goals and contributing to the organization's success.

Take the case of health insurance company Regence, introduced in chapter 1. Regarded in the past as bureaucratic and slow-moving, the organization has undergone a remarkable change over the past several years. Leaders perceive their company as having a central role in driving the transformation of health care in the United States. Regence's people refer to their goal as the Cause, and each one knows its definition: "We will transform health care, reducing the tyranny of health care waste, confusion, and threats for our members and their families." To achieve that goal, the organization has developed several core strategies—long-term, multiyear plans that explain how it intends to foster the Cause. Among these core strategies are: driving a single structure and culture; transforming the health care financing and delivery system; and developing lifetime relationships with members and their families.

Regence employees see this endeavor as bigger than themselves; if the company succeeds in attaining its goals, it will be a key player in a new health care delivery and financing model in the United States. Leaders communicate the cause to all employees and encourage them to join in and to make a commitment to it. One of their mantras is "Live and Own the Cause." CEO Mark Ganz believes that to transform health care, Regence employees first have to transform themselves. He introduced an internal campaign called

"Building a Healthy Future," which emphasizes the need for employees to commit themselves to their own wellness. This campaign illustrates the shift toward greater commitment that Regence leaders are trying to achieve.

Responsibility

The next dimension, responsibility, is the extent to which people feel personally responsible for their work and accountable for solving problems and making decisions.

In chapter 1 we encountered Vodafone Group Plc, the mobile telecommunications company with more than 300 million customers worldwide. Chief executive Vittorio Colao has successfully instilled a climate of high responsibility. He shares an example of his approach:

> Several years ago, we decided to centralize the whole of purchasing within Vodafone. We had been struggling for a while with a very elaborate allocation of who purchases what: this is local, this is regional, this is global, this is right, this is left, and so on. I was in my office with the current head of supply chain management and he was explaining the processes on a flipchart. The drawing on the flipchart had become so complex, it was like snakes crossing each other all across the board.
>
> At some point I said, "Listen, why don't we just make this easy. You get responsibility for the whole thing." We signed a piece of paper that I think he still keeps today. It said, "I, Detlef Schultz, have responsibility for all purchasing for the whole group, and I commit to doing whatever makes sense, locally or globally, without running an oppressive, centralized unit. I understand that if there are a lot of complaints about me I will be fired in twelve months." Signed by him and by me.

I see this as a very simple way to solve problems without having to draw up elaborate organizational blueprints and migration plans. Of course, Schultz had a lot of expertise in this area, but the basic statement was: "I trust you, you do it; and you trust your colleagues, you don't just take away all their responsibility for the sake of centralizing everything." And to this day, I haven't gotten a single complaint. He did a good job.

Recognition

If *recognition* is high, people feel that they're rewarded and recognized for doing good work and that rewards are clearly related to performance excellence (as opposed to seniority, politics, or other factors). The rewards don't necessarily have to be financial; in fact, money may even be counterproductive. Research shows that intrinsic satisfaction in the work provides the most powerful positive reinforcement for behavior.[12] Among external rewards, peer recognition and a sense of belonging and contributing to the group are especially effective.[13]

At Holiday Inn, the implementation team for the large-scale initiative to improve the guest experience was helped by a special group of employees nicknamed "the Green Berets"—after the elite special-forces units of a number of countries' armies. These were people who had passion for the brand and who worked on different aspects of the initiative, such as new recognition programs and selection processes. The Green Berets didn't earn extra pay, even though the efforts were above and beyond their ordinary responsibilities. Instead, they were given green hats and were recognized if they did outstanding work. As Brent Reynolds, owner and general manager of a Holiday Inn in Youngstown, Ohio, states: "We needed to get so much done to accomplish our goals in the timeframes needed—and we didn't have extra payroll to get it done. We couldn't have done what we did without the Green Berets."

Teamwork

Teamwork is the feeling of belonging to an organization characterized by cohesion, mutual support, trust, and pride.

SunGard, the IT services company profiled in chapter 1, provides an example of how teamwork affects climate. For a long time, salespeople from different acquired units within the company had little contact with one another. But when the company rolled out a major learning initiative for the sales force, it deliberately mixed people from different parts of the country in the same classes in order to build camaraderie (similar to the approach we saw used by Waypoint LLC in chapter 2). One result was that salespeople built informal networks of people on whom they can now rely regularly for help in addressing sales challenges back on the job. These networks have broken down barriers and improved climate across Sun-Gard, which in turn has helped foster speed.

Measuring and Managing Climate

Every organization or work unit has a climate profile—that is, a level they have attained on each of the climate dimensions—that can be measured. There is no single, ideal climate profile that is best for every organization. For instance, the military tends to have high clarity and high commitment. Other organizations that prize individual effort may have lower teamwork and higher recognition. Our research indicates, however, that speed of execution is enhanced only when leaders pay attention to all six dimensions. All are important, and all contribute to speed.

There are three steps for managing climate at both the organizational and team levels. This process is based on our findings from several decades of studying climate, and the management practices that affect it, in major corporations around the world.

First, organizations need to conduct a climate survey to understand where they are and where they want to be. Each manager in the organization should receive a report on three issues:

- Employees' perceptions of their team climate in terms of the six climate dimensions

- Employees' perceptions of their manager's use of a set of management practices that support climate

- Employees' ratings of team motivation, performance, and speed of execution (the outcomes of climate)

Second, managers must each construct an action plan to improve climate in their work unit. Finally, organizations need to measure the impact of the improvements and seek further improvements. Often measurement takes the form of regular reassessments of climate and of the results metrics that have been determined up front.

Archstone: Climate and a Commitment to Great Service

Here's a holistic example of how climate drives speed. First we'll look at how climate played a role in this company's overall success; then we'll observe how they coped with a single emergency in which fast execution was critical and climate played a major role.

Archstone is a $1.5 billion real estate company that owns, operates, and develops upscale apartment properties in desirable locations, primarily in coastal North America. The company also has a presence in several European markets. Before going private in late 2007, Archstone was a *Fortune* 1000 company and a member of the S&P 500.

In 2007, the executive leadership team realized that in order to sustain their preeminent position and achieve growth targets, the company needed to transform its relationships with its upscale clientele, especially in its new luxury high-rise properties. The company also needed to respond to increasing competition in traditional markets. Archstone customers are primarily young professionals, a fairly transient population, with an average length of stay of about a year. For this reason, one goal was to attract and retain residents—if not in a particular apartment, then at least in an Archstone property. In response to these challenges, Archstone integrated new leadership talent from the hospitality industry and aligned the organization around a new brand promise: "Great Apartments. Great Service. Guaranteed."

In order to prepare the organization to deliver on their customer promise, the leadership team launched a comprehensive program called "Commitment to GREAT." This program provided managers and frontline associates with the skills and support they needed to deliver excellent customer service at every property. Below are examples of how Archstone used the program to create a customer-centered climate:

- **Clarity:** Leaders at all levels continuously communicated the purpose and benefit of "Commitment to GREAT" in simple terms, such as the acronym GREAT: *g*o the extra mile; *r*eliable and *r*esponsive; *e*mpathize; *a*sk questions and listen; *t*ake ownership.

- **Standards:** Leaders set specific standards of behavior, such as answering phone calls on the first ring or standing when a resident enters the apartment's business office.

- **Commitment:** Leaders tapped into the associates' motivation to serve residents by using Commitment to GREAT as a rallying cry. The associate gatherings often grew quite emotional, as they shared stories about how they had gone the extra mile to help their customers.

- **Responsibility:** Associates were expected to handle resident problems on the local level rather than escalating them to a corporate-based call center. To do so, management allowed each associate to spend up to $1,000 to resolve an issue without having to seek prior approval (for example, if a resident's car was towed inadvertently, an associate could pay the towing company).

- **Recognition:** Leaders made a point of acknowledging extra effort and providing associates with formal and informal recognition and praise frequently.

- **Teamwork:** Leaders reinforced a spirit of teamwork at the properties by visually displaying results and key metrics (for example, an increase in percentage of leased apartments based on local marketing efforts).

Now in its second year of focusing on Commitment to GREAT, Archstone has begun to see definitive results in terms of more effective and engaged employees, increased compliments from residents, and fewer resident issues escalated to management. Even more interesting to us, however, was the speed with which the Commitment to GREAT initiative was executed. The climate Archstone built had a reinforcing effect on the initiative itself, allowing it to move more quickly than usual. The original plan for Commitment to GREAT called for a year of research and planning. The leadership team decided the plan was sound but that it could and must be done much faster; the window of opportunity to make service a competitive differentiator was small. Because they had created high clarity about what needed to be accomplished and a high level of commitment on the team, they agreed they didn't need to spend a year on research to reinforce what they already knew needed to be done. Instead, they reviewed existing data, did fast-paced customer and employee research, adapted best practices from other hospitality organizations, and presented the plan in three months. Next, they brought in all the key decision makers and reviewed the research findings and recommendations. There were many policy decisions that needed to be made (such as the $1,000 discretionary spending limit). Because this was the same leadership team that had already established a climate of team-work, however, they made decisions quickly. Most decisions were completed in a two-day planning meeting—after which each leader went out to "create the buzz."

As a result of accelerating the initiative, Archstone was able to roll out Commitment to GREAT across the entire company within a year, so that customers could experience the benefits that much sooner.

All these results are impressive, but has an improved climate led to increased speed of execution in daily work at Archstone? The following story shows dramatically how it has.

Fires in Yorba Linda. In 2008, Southern California experienced a record number of wildfires, which destroyed over half a million acres and more than two thousand homes. A wildfire that November broke out in Yorba Linda, threatening an Archstone property. The fire was unusually fast-moving—100 feet per second. The fire department arrived at the property and notified the staff of three associates on duty at the time—a leasing consultant, a service technician, and a porter—that they needed to evacuate the residents from all four hundred units, spread across the property in dozens of buildings.

How much time did they have? The firefighters' answer: fifteen minutes.

The staff sprang into action, banging on doors and recruiting residents to bang on their neighbors' doors, until all the apartments were vacant. One associate even ran into a woman's apartment to rescue her dog as flames began to engulf the building.

Before it was over, two buildings had burned to the ground, displacing fifteen families. The associates quickly relocated all fifteen of those families to other Archstone properties.

When asked what helped them prepare for such an emergency, an associate said it was their "Commitment to GREAT," which focused on residents' needs and delivering superior service—even during a natural disaster. This story illustrates how the dimensions of climate—especially commitment, responsibility, and teamwork—become especially important when results, or even lives, depend on speed. A positive climate at that Archstone property in Yorba Linda made the difference between a fast, fluid, effective response to a crisis and what might have been an uncoordinated, slow, or panicked response.

If there is such a thing as a magic wand to create strategic speed in everyday execution, climate is it. (See "Managing Climate: Reduced Time to Value, Increased Value over Time" for a summary of how organizations described in this chapter achieved results.) No other concept is so simple—so apparently "soft"—and yet has such a powerful effect on teams' and organizations' ability to execute, and execute fast. What makes climate so powerful is that leaders can change it fairly easily, and the resulting changes have a strong impact on people's level of motivation and performance. Climate is a true lever for increasing speed in organizations.

Archimedes said, "Give me a lever long enough and a fulcrum on which to place it, and I shall move the world." We say, "Get yourself some leaders who understand climate and an action plan to address it, and you'll move your entire organization—fast."

MANAGING CLIMATE: REDUCED TIME TO VALUE, INCREASED VALUE OVER TIME

- Tata Sky, six months into its existence, asked Nielsen to conduct a customer satisfaction survey and compare it to other companies in the telecom and consumer durables sectors. To Nielsen's great surprise, Tata Sky scored higher on customer satisfaction than any other firm in those sectors worldwide—a remarkable achievement for a brand just six months old.

- Abbott Vascular China increased customer satisfaction dramatically, reduced employee turnover by 85 percent, and created a new "buzz" in the market over an eighteen-month period. As a result, the business went from posting a net loss to achieving 75 percent year-over-year revenue growth.

- Archstone implemented its customer service initiative, including training twenty-five hundred associates, a full year ahead of schedule. As its local residential staff gained competence and authority to handle customer issues, there was a 90 percent drop in escalations of complaints to their central call center, which was subsequently disbanded.

How Are You Doing on Managing Climate?

You can use this quick assessment to size up your personal effectiveness at managing climate and identify opportunities for increasing strategic speed.

Scale: 1 = to a very small extent; 5 = to a very great extent

I focus not just on business results (lagging indicators) but on the climate dimensions that lead to results.   1   2   3   4   5

I conduct regular climate "temperature checks" to ensure that people are motivated.   1   2   3   4   5

I have defined the kind of climate that would best support our business objectives.   1   2   3   4   5

I have informal discussions about climate with my employees and peers.   1   2   3   4   5

I seek to learn how my employees view my management practices.   1   2   3   4   5

I have specific goals and a plan for shaping the climate of my work group.   1   2   3   4   5

I convey the importance of climate to our senior leaders and explain how it drives results.   1   2   3   4   5

To obtain your score on managing climate, add your ratings and divide by 7: _____

Interpretation:

- If your score is less than 3.0, you have an opportunity to improve on managing climate.

- If your score is between 3.0 and 4.0, you're doing a good job on managing climate, but you may see some specific opportunities for improvement.

- If your score is greater than 4.0, you're doing an excellent job on managing climate and should share your knowledge and tips with other leaders.

SIX

Leaders Cultivate Experience

T HE FINAL LEADERSHIP PRACTICE—and one that, like managing climate, helps accelerate everyday execution—is *cultivating experience.* In our Global Speed Survey, we found that one of the factors differentiating faster companies from slower companies is "Leaders who learn and improve from experience continuously." Cultivating experience increases *clarity* by allowing people time to discuss goals and reflect on progress toward them; increases *unity* by expecting each individual to have a perspective, offer insights, and contribute to team learning; and increases *agility* by enabling people to learn from experience and apply lessons quickly to emerging problems.

It's no secret that experienced people and teams can move faster than inexperienced ones. There's an old story about Pablo Picasso that speaks to this truth. He was sketching in a smoky corner of a Paris café when a woman approached him. "Oh, Monsieur Picasso . . . the great artist!" she exclaimed. "I so admire your work. *S'il vous plaît*, will you sketch my portrait?"

Picasso agreed. He took up his pad and, after studying the woman for a moment, dashed off her portrait with a single stroke of his pencil. He handed the paper to her and turned back to his glass of absinthe.

"Monsieur, it's wonderful!" she gushed. "How much do I owe you?"

"Ten thousand francs, Madame."

"Ten thousand francs?!" she shrieked. "Monsieur Picasso, it took you but a few seconds!"

He replied: "Madame, to be able to do *that*—it took me my entire life."

Well-Cultivated Experience Drives Speed

A great artist with forty years of practice under his belt can do a high-quality sketch in moments. A well-functioning team with a year of experience working together can complete a project faster than a newly formed team. An organization that takes full advantage of its employees' and teams' experience will move faster than one that does not. The big caveat, though, is that merely "experiencing" a lot of events doesn't necessarily result in an increase in knowledge, skill, or speed. Plenty of people like to paint and do it for decades, yet they never become the next Picasso. People and teams in organizations have experiences all day long, but that doesn't guarantee an increase in their performance. Someone with twenty years of experience could have the equivalent of one year of experience repeated nineteen times. Just "being there"—though it may have worked for Peter Sellers in the film of that name—isn't sufficient.

Experience is only helpful to strategic speed if it is *cultivated*. There are several definitions of *cultivate*, and all are relevant: to foster growth; to improve by labor, care, or study; to refine; to further or encourage. When we think of cultivating experience, we think about experience being brought into view, made significant, shared, encouraged to endure, and harnessed so that it contributes power to organizational endeavors. When experience isn't cultivated, it remains unnoticed, insignificant, private, and evanescent; in short, it makes no contribution to individual or organizational success.

For a metaphor, think of green energy—solar, wind, and hydro power. Green energy is everywhere: all around us the sun is shining, the wind is blowing, water is flowing. In order to create power for human needs, however, that energy needs to be captured and harnessed. When it is, it can heat and cool houses, water farms, and make cars go; when it isn't, it passes by without being put to use. Similarly, when experience in organizations isn't captured and harnessed, it goes to waste and speed suffers. (Remember the situation at SmartCom: the billing-system experts had been outsourced, many of them had left altogether, and the original code hadn't been documented. All that experience had blown or trickled away.) In addition, failure to make use of experience often means leaders must fall back on other sources of energy to get things done faster, such as streamlining processes, installing technologies, and plain old yelling and shouting. Most of those other sources of energy are neither as sustainable nor as powerful as properly cultivated experience can be.

Traditionally, leaders have been well aware that smart, skilled, experienced employees and teams are critical to an organization's success. And, traditionally, they have relied mostly on one method of increasing the skills and knowledge of their employees: formal training. They have sent their employees (and have gone themselves) to classes, away from the job, taught by instructors. In recent years, some of those face-to-face training programs have been replaced by e-learning courses and instructor-led virtual classes, but the model is fundamentally the same: whether it's for days or for hours, people are sent off the playing field to learn something—and then everyone hopes that, once back on the job, they will (a) remember what they learned, (b) translate and apply it, and (c) keep on doing it. Yet study after study indicates that 70 to 90 percent of workplace learning happens informally on the job, while only 10 to 30 percent happens in formal settings, whether face to face or virtual.[1] Typically, when people are asked to describe their most memorable learning experience, they don't mention a class; they mention a highly challenging or even painful situation in their work or personal life. Real-world experience is, apparently, the teacher most of us remember best. As Mark Twain put it, "A man who carries a cat by the tail learns something he can learn in no other way."

Though formal training certainly has its place, some leaders are starting to recognize the enormous untapped potential that exists in the experience that "floats around" their organizations all day long. How can they harness that experience and use it to increase knowledge, skill, and speed? How can they better channel and direct the many opportunities for learning that arise constantly in people's daily tasks, conversations, and projects? How can they ensure that the insight people gain from experience endures, grows, and gets applied to the work—instead of blowing away like dust in the wind?

Leaders as Cultivators

As with all the other keys to strategic speed, it is primarily *leaders* who cultivate experience in their organizations and networks—or fail to do so. Perhaps not surprisingly, there is no precise word in English for "a leader who is good at drawing forth and harnessing people's experience and using it to increase knowledge, skill, and speed across the organization." *Teacher* might be a good word, but *teacher* connotes someone who possesses his or her own expert knowledge of something and can convey that knowledge to others. We believe cultivating experience is something different: a practice based less on articulating one's own point of view and more on making others' points of view visible, keen, and valuable.

There's also the word *facilitator*, but we believe that's too narrow a term as well. *Facilitator* connotes someone who orchestrates conversations so that they're smoother or more productive; *facilitate* literally means "to make easier." Skilled facilitation is nothing to sneeze at, but we aren't talking just about helping people conduct more productive discussions and meetings.

We use *cultivator* as the term for a leader who makes the most of experience in his or her organization. Cultivators don't only teach and don't only facilitate; they take the experience, knowledge, and insights that are latent in individuals and teams and actively draw them out, making them more productive and powerful. Cultivators have teachable points of view and don't hesitate to articulate them; more than that, though, they help others develop and articulate their own insightful points of view and apply them to the work at hand. Cultivators capture and harness the "green energy" of experience and wisdom that floats around the organization and that, without their help, tends to go unappreciated and unused.

One of the principles we've developed from our years of research is "Provide learners with a balance of challenge and support." The key to becoming a great cultivator is to give strong—and equal—attention to those two aspects of people's development. (And to do so *actively*—see "Is Becoming 'Learner-Centric' the Answer?") First, learning is most effective when learners are highly challenged. Computer-based simulations that demand performance (such as conducting surgery on a simulated patient) are better at fostering learning than reading about medical procedures in a book or online. And, as we noted above, when people are asked to name a time when they learned a lot, they usually name a highly challenging situation. On the other hand, challenging situations often generate excessive stress, which can interfere with learning. Individuals

IS BECOMING "LEARNER-CENTRIC" THE ANSWER?

One might think that cultivating experience is mostly a matter of putting the responsibility and tools for learning in the hands of individuals and letting them get on with it. Today we hear a lot about organizations becoming "learner-centric"; experts claim that given the right conditions and the right knowledge-management technologies, people will be self-directed when it comes to building their knowledge and skills. Much is made of social media, the tools that allow individuals to form and manage online networks, generate and publish content on their own, and find almost any piece of information in seconds. Much is written about the entrance into the workforce of new generations, who, it is said, prefer to be free to seek out experts and resources on their own. Leaders are exhorted to stop being so controlling, to let people learn what they want to learn.

We're not so sure that's the answer. Though there's no doubt that social media tools and younger employees constitute new challenges for leaders, we've observed that effective cultivators today do just what great teachers have been doing for thousands of years: They demand much, and they care much. They challenge their students, and they support them.

need to feel safe to explore new ideas and actions; they need support in order to take the risks inherent in learning and changing. The situations that create the greatest learning, that cultivate experience the most, are those that provide a high level of challenge *and* a high level of support. An analogy is a trapeze artist who is able to experiment with daring maneuvers, knowing that he has a net beneath him.

We saw in chapter 4 that leaders shouldn't get out of the driver's seat once they've introduced a strategic initiative and gained people's buy-in; the best leaders, rather, stay in the game and drive execution. Similarly, leaders shouldn't stay above the fray when it comes to encouraging learning and harnessing experience. If, intending to be learner-centric, you put "Learning"—like a nicely wrapped gift—into the hands of your employees and turn your attention to more pressing things, you'll likely find that the recipients have quickly judged the gift to be attractive but not very practical. They'll stuff Learning in the back of the closet and turn *their* attention to more pressing things, too.

Think of your best teachers, coaches, or mentors from the past—those who really helped you grow. Did they leave it up to you to direct your learning? Did they merely "create a space" for learning, give you some tools, and let you decide what you felt like learning that day? Did they let you evaluate your own work? Or, did they make it perfectly clear that (a) you could do better, and (b) you really *could* do better—that they believed completely in your ability to reach a higher standard and were committed to helping you get there?

Levels of Experience

We suggest that leaders work on cultivating experience at three levels:

- **For yourself:** Be a good cultivator of your own experience. Model the attitudes and behaviors for others.

- **For individuals:** Help individual employees and colleagues cultivate their knowledge, skills, judgment, and insight— both in formal coaching conversations and informally.

- **For teams:** Work with teams to put processes and practices in place that develop their collective knowledge, skills, judgment, and insight.

People have asked us if there's also an organizational level. Our answer is: yes and no. Yes, organizational systems and processes— such as reward and recognition systems, knowledge management systems, and performance management processes—can make cultivating experience either easier or more difficult. But as a cultivator, you want to focus your attention mainly on the people and groups with whom you interact. Though creating a "learning organization" is a worthy goal, it's actually *individuals* and *teams* who learn—not organizations. Even CEOs, if they want to become good cultivators, will find their opportunities primarily in conversations, meetings, and work sessions with the people and teams that make up the organization, not in the knowledge management systems they install or the speeches they broadcast. (For an example of how one CEO does this, see below, where we share the ideas of Vodafone's Vittorio Colao.)

Let's listen to several leaders' insights on these three levels of cultivating experience.

For Yourself: "What Could I Be Doing Differently?"

Claudine Wolfe is managing director and global head of leadership development and learning technologies for Morgan Stanley. She was on the team that got Morgan Stanley University up and running in four months and, in the process, transformed learning and development at that company. Here she describes how she cultivated her own experience in order to be successful during that initiative, especially in the many situations in which she found herself out of her comfort zone:

> I was constantly self-reflecting and self-managing, asking, "How are you handling that? What would you do differently?" I tried to emotionally disconnect myself and look at it from an objective practitioner's point of view, thinking about how I would actually be advising myself. Almost saying, "If I were my own coach, what advice would I be giving myself in this transition and experience that I'm going through?" I think in a lot of ways that helped me stay the course and stay focused—still passionate and emotionally invested, but in a way that didn't create stress and anxiety and that allowed me to achieve what we needed to achieve.

Wolfe also talks about the importance of soliciting feedback: "I think it takes a tremendous amount of courage to constantly keep asking for feedback. In one of my previous roles, we were doing a reorg, and the team had the courage to keep asking for feedback: 'What should we be doing differently? What could I be doing differently? How do you think that went?' It's not only about asking for feedback, but being able to embrace it in a way that demonstrates you're open to it and doing something about it."

For Individuals: Making Invisible Behavior Visible

There are many techniques by which leaders can cultivate experience with direct reports or other individuals whom they coach. All of them are essentially about helping people build self-observation, practice, and reflection into their activities and projects. If well designed, these methods can be more powerful than traditional training classes. Steve Barry, senior manager of strategic marketing at

The Forum Corporation, provides an example of a technique that he's used:

> Say you have an employee, call him Leonard, a first-line manager who needs to improve his communication skills. Traditionally, you'd send Leonard to a two- or three-day class where he'd be lectured on the importance of listening and asking various types of questions. He'd probably do a role-play or two. When he returned, you'd assume that he had learned what he needed to learn and that your work was done.
>
> Today, you might try a different method: You ask Leonard to attend a brief class or webinar where he learns about the concepts behind good communication. You then have him record his next conference call and have it transcribed. Together, you sit down and go through the transcript. The two of you can see, with your own eyes, how many times Leonard asked questions rather than advocating a position, what types of questions they were, how long he talked compared with others, and how many times he interrupted someone. People often don't realize what their speech patterns are, but examining a transcript makes it very real.
>
> Coaching techniques like that, built into daily work, can make invisible behavior visible and increase people's motivation to learn and change.

For Teams: The Pursuit of New Possibilities in Small Groups

Amy Edmondson is the Novartis Professor of Leadership and Management at Harvard Business School. Much of her research has focused on how organizations learn and, specifically, how *teams* in organizations learn. Edmondson has identified practices that help leaders promote team learning without sacrificing short-term performance. In an interview with Sarah Jane Gilbert, she talks about her view of learning and teams:[2]

> I suggest that organizations learn through the learning of groups within the organizations. So, an organization's ability to learn—again, to improve its performance through better knowledge and action—is shaped by the interactions of individuals, typically situated within small groups or teams. When these groups make appropriate changes in how they do their work—driven by both group and organizational goals—an organization maintains or enhances its effectiveness in a changing world. Organizational learning can be seen as a process of cascading team learning activities—independently carried out but interdependent in their impact on company performance.
>
> Different types of teams or groups face different learning needs and challenges. A leadership team may face the need to make strategic decisions in a shifting landscape of possibilities, while a product development team struggles to understand customers' changing needs and to invent new ways to serve them, and a production team seeks to improve its work process. Seen in this way, managers have two jobs. One is to become great team leaders who encourage open discussion, trial and error, and the pursuit of new possibilities in the small groups they directly influence. The other is to work hard to build organizations conducive to extraordinary teamwork and learning behaviors throughout the organization.

The locus for learning isn't the organization; it's the individual or the team. When leaders cultivate experience at the individual and team levels, however, the effects can ripple across an entire organization.

Vodafone Group: How One "Cultivator" Impacts an Entire Organization

Here's how Vodafone Group chief executive Vittorio Colao uses storytelling with teams and individuals to create cross-pollination of ideas and increase speed across his global organization:

> The beauty of operating in twenty-plus different countries across five different continents is that we have an ability to share what works, what doesn't, and new ideas which go a bit beyond—and sometimes against—hierarchical or established communication flows. I have a background in consulting, and the lesson that you learn when you're a consultant is that you talk to whoever has the best competence, regardless of hierarchy, role, or country. We have fantastic examples of ideas, products, and innovations that have started out in one market almost by mistake and then spread to the rest of the world.
>
> In order to share information like that, you need two infrastructures. One is a kind of communication infrastructure, which can exist in a variety of formats—like an intranet, forums, distribution lists. The other is a *personal* infrastructure, which is really about knowing who does what, who is good, and who has great ideas. It's about personal interaction between people who may be thousands of kilometers away, but when they have a problem they ask, "Who is the prepaid expert? Who is the DSL expert? How did Italy launch the integrated mobile fixed DSL station, and why don't I launch it the same way? Who is the genius who does advertising for the younger kids of Portugal? Let me give him a call and ask him how to do the same thing in Australia." This personal infrastructure is the difficult part, because a technological infrastructure for the sake of sharing content—we all can deploy that. Making sure the neurons are applied to the bits is the more difficult part.

Colao goes on to say that his main method for developing a "personal infrastructure" is storytelling:

> I'm the storyteller of the company. I go around saying, "In this country I've seen this," or "They have done that well." One of the privileges of being the CEO is that I visit nearly all our markets each year, and I always do three things: one is a session with the young talent, one is a session with the local manager and team, and one is a larger session with the employees in which I ask them to show me what they've done very well and are proud of. Then in my next speech in the next country, it's easy for me to say, "In Germany they've done very well with social graphs" (where we map customers' social interactions), and they immediately say, "Oh, we do the same," and they describe what *they* do. And then, it's almost natural for them to call their colleagues in Germany the next day and say, "Can you show us?"
>
> It sounds a bit passé, but there's nothing like telling anecdotes, indicating that you like what you've seen in New Zealand or Egypt or wherever, to create a desire to emulate and to initiate contact.

How to Cultivate Experience

In our study of what leaders do in order to capture experience in their organizations and put it to work, four themes or competences emerged:

- Conscious practice
- Openness
- Reflection in action
- Experimentation

To increase strategic speed, leaders should develop these "CORE" competences at the different levels we've discussed: in themselves, in their individual employees and colleagues, and in teams. On the following pages we'll describe each competence and what it looks like in action.

Conscious Practice

Capturing and harnessing experience is difficult. It requires continuous objective analysis of one's own behaviors, thinking, and emotions in relation to the results obtained. We call this competence *conscious* practice for a reason: individuals must bring experience to the forefront of their mind during daily activities, just as they must consciously seek opportunities in which to practice.

Conscious practice is similar to deliberate practice, a concept coined by psychologist K. Anders Ericsson of Florida State University and made popular by Geoffrey Colvin and Malcolm Gladwell.[3] Deliberate practice is a method of actively learning from experience, with emphasis on the experience. It involves setting specific goals, obtaining immediate feedback, and concentrating as much on technique as on outcomes. Deliberate practice drives expert performance. According to Ericsson and his colleagues, "It's activity that's explicitly intended to improve performance, that reaches for objectives just beyond one's level of competence, provides feedback on results and involves high levels of repetition."[4]

Conscious practice incorporates many of the same tenets and principles of deliberate practice. Goals, practice, feedback: all are key. The difference is that, while Ericsson cites many kinesthetic examples, conscious practice is exclusively related to the cognitive activities that are at the heart of the jobs performed by today's knowledge workers. In conscious practice, people identify goals with respect to improving their knowledge, skills, and behaviors, and they practice to achieve those goals using in-the-moment learning.

Conscious practice is not about finding the time to "go away and practice"; it's about intentionally integrating practice into everyday work. At SunGard, we found an example of a leader fostering conscious practice on a team. SVP Jim Olson leads an inside sales unit that sells SunGard Availability Services to smaller clients, helping them mitigate risks to their data caused by security breaches, natural disasters, and the like. When he originally conceived of the idea for the unit, the common wisdom was that this type of sale was too complex to be done by phone; it could only be done through face-to-face sales calls. Olson thought otherwise. He simplified the sales process and designed three sales calls: a brief introductory call to generate interest; a thirty-minute call, accompanied by a sales engineer, to assess customer needs in more detail; and a sixty-minute call to develop a proposal, followed by the close. In the course of their daily work, sales reps now focus on getting better at each specific type of call. They know exactly what skills are required for each type, and they know what constitutes success for each type; so, after each call, they can reflect on how well they did and how they might do better. Sales reps work in a call center where they have quick and easy access to their sales managers, to supporting information, and to other reps. This is an ideal environment for practicing how to handle the different types of calls, gaining immediate feedback, and brainstorming sales strategies. By simplifying and clarifying the sales process and fostering conscious practice, Olson and his team not only have proved that complex sales can be done over the phone but also have cut sales cycle time by 50 percent—from nine months down to about four and a half.

Openness

Another strong theme uncovered by our research is the ability to keep an open mind. A leader with an open mind encourages people to put unfinished or imperfect ideas forward so they can be built upon by others, to bring bad news forward early so it can be addressed, and to suggest big ideas, not just incremental improvements.

Another type of openness is the ability to observe everything around you, piece together new patterns, and take action based on those patterns. Mohan Nair, executive vice president of marketing at Regence, the health insurance company, says, "You need to have compound eyes." An example of this was when employees at Regence listened to customers and noticed a trend of problems coalescing around parenting. While parenting hasn't traditionally been considered a health issue, these employees believed that it had health care implications; increased stress, for example, might negatively affect couples with new babies. Regence enhanced its customer Web sites to provide further education and support related to parenting. Customers valued the effort greatly, and Regence won awards for these programs. A closed-minded leader would have said, "Parenting is not a health issue" and shut down the idea; the Regence leaders, however, encouraged employees to use their "compound eyes" to see beyond a traditional definition of health and make new connections that ultimately added tremendous value for customers.

Tata Sky's CEO Vikram Kaushik speaks about openness as he describes his organization's race to start India's first direct-to-home satellite TV company:

> First of all, we've never allowed anybody to develop tunnel vision on what they were doing. It was not about the here-and-now all the time. I think every member of the team went overseas to look at the way it was being done in BSkyB or Sky Italia or Foxtel or wherever. Secondly, because Star [our media-company partner] was involved out of Hong Kong, there was a fair amount of cross-fertilization of ideas between that center and here. I was traveling to Hong Kong once in three

months myself, to attend meetings on what was happening to the broadcast industry. It always kept my mind fresh on the big issues.

Finally, Kaushik says, "I think it was all about keeping the windows open—the old Mahatma Gandhi saying about letting many cultures' winds blow. We kept that alive."

Reflection in Action

People learn by doing and by thinking about what they've done. Reflection generates lessons for future action. It allows people to examine experiences, to find meaning in them, and to generate new insights and knowledge. When we're faced with little time and an urgent need for results, however, we tend to sacrifice reflection in favor of "act, act, and act some more." The irony is that nonstop action leads to zero cultivation of experience and, in the end, less speed.

In our survey, we asked leaders to tell us which of these two statements described their initiatives best: "Despite the workload, people on the team(s) found the time to review how the work is going" or, "There was simply no time for reflection among the team(s)." Leaders in the faster organizations tended to choose the former statement; leaders in the slower organizations chose the latter. Similarly, when asked to choose between "The teams captured and communicated lessons learned from the initiative," and "After the initiative the teams moved on to other assignments without a formal debrief," leaders in the faster companies were far more likely to choose the former statement.

There are many ways for people to build reflection into their work and to help others do so. To build reflection into the work of teams, consider after-action reviews, a "method for extracting lessons from one event or project and applying them to others."[5]

They're a way to ensure that lessons from past initiatives help people avoid future problems. For example, reviewing the failure of the REMAC (Regence Membership and Claims; see chapter 1) initiative was one of the first things Regence did as it launched a new effort to develop a common set of processes and systems for the consortium. For his capstone MBA project, executive vice president of health care operations Bill Barr studied reams of documents and provided an assessment of why the REMAC project failed and how to avoid those failures in the future. The key, however, is that Barr's team didn't end their review there. Shortly into the new initiative, they held a *mid*-action review. Barr realized with horror that the same problems that had caused the first failure were cropping up again. With a focus on performance rather than blame, Barr set about correcting the behaviors and processes. He later commissioned a team not only to set up regular after-action reviews, but to make the learnings available to the rest of the company.

After-action reviews also yield benefits *before* they are conducted: When people know that an after-action review is planned, it heightens their awareness and attention during the planning and alignment phases as well as during the project.[6] When people know they'll have to explain what worked and what didn't, they ask leaders to state goals and intent very clearly in the beginning, to eliminate as much ambiguity as possible. Conducting BARs, DARs, and AARs (before-, during-, and after-action reviews) is a good way to cultivate experience and increase speed in daily work.

Experimentation

In *Essentials of Balanced Scorecard*, Mohan Nair of Regence notes that strategic initiatives typically flow through the following cycle:[7]

- **Trigger:** Something happens that triggers awareness of the need for change.

- **Education:** People personally experience what the strategic shift would feel like.

- **Pilot:** Starting small, the organization experiments with the new processes and behaviors.

- **Enterprise:** The new strategy is rolled out enterprise-wide.

According to Nair's research, 99 percent of missteps and slowdowns occur because people jump from trigger to enterprise (rollout), skipping the education and pilot phases, where the most learning happens. Nair contends, "Education before execution is a big deal. The initiatives that succeed include this step. However, education doesn't mean just formal education or learning. It means giving people the tools, and then letting them experience the new way."

Experimentation starts with an environment in which new approaches are valued at least as highly as reliable approaches. In our survey, leaders in faster companies chose the statement "The team(s) experimented frequently with new ways of doing things" to describe their initiatives. Leaders in slower companies tended to choose the statement "The team(s) followed reliable processes for doing the work."

John Agresto of the American University of Iraq has taken an experimental approach to the endeavor of setting up that institution. "I made it a policy at the start that we would have no policies," Agresto states. "No one could come to me and say, 'But you did it this way last year,' or 'But you did it that way for Joe, why not me?' We had no policies, only practices; we set no precedents. Everything was an experiment and subject to change. *Everything*. Over time, we'd grow to have 'policies,' but not at first. Nothing was set in stone; we would, in time, codify what worked and not be held captive to what didn't."

In many of our interviews at Regence, people referred to their business environment as a laboratory or Petri dish. An experimental mind-set permeates the entire organization. (We also heard this "laboratory" theme at Morgan Stanley and elsewhere.) The most senior executives view execution as a continual cycle of experimentation, consisting of practice, assessment, reflection, and more practice.

Conscious practice, openness, reflection, and experimentation are the techniques good cultivators use to harness experience. But we also like the way Mohan Nair puts it, very concisely: "It's all about being stupid," he says. "The more stupid you are, the faster you learn."

Irving Oil: The Power of Cultivated Experience

Our final example in this chapter shows how one company turned its store managers into cultivators of experience and reaped great rewards as a result.

Irving Oil is a third-generation family-owned business located in Atlantic Canada and the northeastern United States. Fort Reliance is its parent company. Irving Oil refines and markets gasoline, diesel, home heating fuel, and jet fuel and operates a network of gas-station convenience stores under the Irving brand. It has established itself as an industry leader, operating Canada's largest refinery and producing fuels that are years ahead of environmental regulations. In 2003, the company was recognized for its early introduction of low-sulfur gasoline and became the first oil company ever to receive a U.S. EPA Clean Air Excellence award.

In the early 2000s, Irving Oil established ambitious financial targets that build on its core strengths in customer service and supply chain management while also requiring increased capability to manage change. Reaching these targets would require an unprecedented level of engagement from all the company's managers and employees. One of the major initiatives launched was an effort to enhance the Irving brand. The goal: to ensure that Irving Oil delivers consistent, differentiated, and valuable experiences to customers—whether in the company's service stations, convenience stores, home heating services business, or commercial fuel depots.

The Forum Corporation helped Irving Oil's leaders design new customer experiences for their various customers and delivery channels, among them the company's two hundred convenience stores across Canada and the northeastern United States. The key to the whole initiative was the store managers; they were the ones who'd need to grasp the new behaviors required of employees, coach and support their employees intensively, and ensure that the new customer promise was actually coming to life in the stores. First, all the store managers came together as a group to learn a coaching model (as at Waypoint and other companies, this proved an effective mechanism for increasing unity); then a cadre of Forum coaches went back with the managers to their stores to provide real-time, in-store coaching. One of the coaches, Richard Meyer, describes the extraordinary power of the process:

> We spent several half days or full days in each store. Our main job was to help the managers become coaches of their employees; they needed to coach and build commitment to a new way of relating to customers. One of the things we had prescribed as part of their coaching process was a daily "lineup"—a meeting of the store employees, led by the manager. We'd help the managers prepare in advance, observe them, and give them feedback afterward. The biggest challenge for them was making the meeting interactive—making it about learning, rather than just reciting the latest policies from headquarters. They needed to move from being a talking head to engaging with their employees.

Meyer describes how the managers were helped with one-on-one coaching, as well:

> The one-on-one coaching process we taught them was about being a thinking partner. This was really new for them. The vast majority only knew the "dirt-filled sandwich" method of giving feedback—you know: "Oh, you're doing so well, now let me tell you what you did wrong—oh, but you're doing such a great job." We helped the managers move from a tell-tell-tell mode to being real thinking partners to their staff.
>
> For many of them, it was difficult to be asking questions and keeping their mouths shut [when they felt the need to jump in]. I remember one manager, I'll call her Stacy, had a real breakthrough: I was sitting with her and one of her employees as she conducted a coaching session on the back steps of the store—that's where most of these conversations would happen, out in back of the store, not sitting down formally in the manager's office. Stacy would ask a question; the employee would begin talking; Stacy would look at me; and she would literally grit her teeth. She'd look back at the employee, look at me again, and you could tell she badly wanted to start talking, but she'd just grit her teeth and stay quiet! After a minute, all three of us burst out laughing, because it was clearly so hard for Stacy—and yet, in the end, she was so proud of herself, and her employees were proud of her, too. She actually changed her behavior.

Each store manager was given a box filled with instructions and supplies for coaching conversations, short exercises, and games and challenges that they could use in the daily lineup or in one-on-ones with their employees to increase professionalism and situational judgment. Many of the activities focused on getting employees to share their ideas about providing better customer service or dealing with real challenges. Meyer says that the new approach to coaching elicited a wealth of great ideas and insights from employees: "Once they saw they had permission to do what they thought was best for the customer, and that their ideas were valued, innovation really took off. Stories of employees going the extra mile for customers got posted and shared, both within each store and across the company. The employees felt fantastic about what they could achieve. Now, even if there's a new store manager or if a manager backslides, the employees will still carry the new ways forward. They've seen what they can do."

The results speak for themselves. After the initiative was launched in the pilot locations, store manager skills improved, employee loyalty went up, customer satisfaction increased, and same-store sales jumped. All this in less than a year, and without large investments in advertising or fancy marketing systems.

Like green energy, cultivation of experience can yield big results (see "Cultivating Experience: Reduced Time to Value, Increased Value over Time"). To fail to harness your people's experience is to waste one of your greatest, most sustainable resources for driving strategic speed. In contrast, when the experience of myriad individuals is drawn forth, shared, and applied, it contributes enormous power to team and organizational endeavors. As one of the Irving Oil executives put it, "The results can be seen in a thousand small changes and a thousand actions. All add up to a big impact."

CULTIVATING EXPERIENCE: REDUCED TIME TO VALUE, INCREASED VALUE OVER TIME

- In the fiscal year ended March 31, 2009, Vodafone Group increased revenue by 15.6 percent, operating profit by 16.7 percent, and earnings per share by 37.4 percent—this despite a worldwide recession that saw many companies' results falling by double digits. At the same time they accelerated a £1 billion cost reduction program, delivering 65 percent of the reductions within two years, ahead of plan.

- Regence has improved its overall speed to market significantly. In 2008, they launched three new products; previously, they had launched one new product every three years. They also achieved a dramatic culture shift in just three years—much faster than the seven to ten years generally needed for such deep changes.

- At Irving Oil, the following results were achieved in the pilot locations in less than a year: store manager skills improved 33 percent; employee loyalty went up 16 percent; customer satisfaction increased by 20 percent; and customer loyalty and same-store sales each went up 10 percent.

How Are You Doing on Cultivating Experience?

You can use this quick assessment to size up your personal effectiveness at cultivating experience and identify opportunities for increasing strategic speed.

Scale: 1 = to a very small extent; 5 = to a very great extent

I foster people's growth by challenging and supporting
them in their learning.   1   2   3   4   5

I give employees opportunities to practice the changes
in behavior they need to make.   1   2   3   4   5

I seek to turn pressure, feedback, and conflict into
facilitators of learning.   1   2   3   4   5

I have established ways of reflecting regularly—such as scheduling
reflection time or keeping a journal.   1   2   3   4   5

I have instituted practices such as after-action reviews
that foster reflection in teams.   1   2   3   4   5

I have a "laboratory" mind-set and treat projects as
opportunities to experiment and learn.   1   2   3   4   5

I help people capture and share learning during projects,
rather than waiting until the end.   1   2   3   4   5

To obtain your score on cultivating experience, add your ratings and divide by 7: _____

Interpretation:

- If your score is less than 3.0, you have an opportunity to improve on cultivating experience.

- If your score is between 3.0 and 4.0, you're doing a good job on cultivating experience, but you may see some specific opportunities for improvement.

- If your score is greater than 4.0, you're doing an excellent job on cultivating experience and should share your knowledge and tips with other leaders.

SEVEN

Tools for Achieving Strategic Speed

S PEED IS NOT ABOUT concocting brilliant strategies; it's about leaders who know how to accelerate *execution* of strategies by adopting the right mind-set and taking the right actions—actions that are focused on mobilizing people. Strategic speed is where urgency meets execution, and that means you don't need to go into a bunker and spend months doing analyses and drawing up complex plans in order to see improvement. Rather, organizations can get immediate traction by equipping every one of their leaders to think and behave in speed-promoting ways.

As a leader, however, you may be wondering: where do I begin? The four tools in this chapter provide a guide:

1. Begin by seeking opportunities to deploy the Time/Value Assessment in your work. This tool, which you use to take quick periodic "readings" of employees, teams, or projects

over the course of several months, will give you a visual sense of the strategic speed (reduced time to value and increased value over time) that is being achieved within your business unit.

2. Next, look for opportunities to deploy the Team Survey. This ten-minute questionnaire, which you send out to members of your team or business unit, will tell you exactly how clear, unified, and agile they feel—and why. When you use the survey in conjunction with the Strategic Speedometer that appears in chapter 2 you'll get a detailed picture of where your business unit stands on the three people factors of clarity, unity, and agility, and you'll be able to identify key trouble spots.

3. To gain more precise information on what's slowing you down and what's moving you forward, use the Leadership Profile to diagnose your business unit's weaknesses and strengths in the four leadership practices: affirming strategies, driving initiatives, managing climate, and cultivating experience.

4. Finally, use the Speed Matrix to help you pull all the information together and select your top-priority actions to mobilize people and accelerate execution.

The Time/Value Assessment: Are Your People and Projects Achieving Strategic Speed?

In chapter 1 we explained the two metrics that define strategic speed: reducing time to value and increasing value over time. We contrasted this view of speed with the mistaken view that speed is merely about getting from A to B in record time. Determining time to value and value over time doesn't require complex calculations. All you have to do is complete the following assessment of your people, teams, and/or projects about once a month. If you take regular "readings," you'll be able to plot a curve on a noise-value chart—similar to a temperature chart—and get a visual sense of time to value and value over time within your business unit. Your chart might look something like figure 7-1.

Taking regular readings and plotting these curves will give you an idea of how quickly your people, teams, and projects are rising above the noise-value line (time to value) and, just as important, whether they are *staying* above the line (value over time). You'll get a sense of which people, teams, and projects are exemplars of strategic speed and which ones are decidedly not. If you complete the assessment regularly and broadly (for example, with every new hire or every initiative you lead), you'll also get a sense of the typical curves for individuals, teams, and projects within your business unit; you can then use those curves as a baseline for comparisons. Identifying the patterns that exist across your group is more useful than plotting a curve for just one individual or initiative.

FIGURE 7-1

Sample noise-value chart

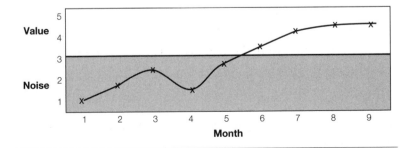

The assessment can be used to assess the value being created by:

- An *individual employee* or *associate*, especially one who has recently been hired or has stepped into a new role or assignment

- A *team*, *task force*, or *work group*, especially one that is newly formed or has acquired a new leader or members

- A *project* or *initiative*

Each of these contexts has its own unique set of six questions, shown below. Each set takes one to two minutes to answer. Ideally you would complete the assessment every month from the time an individual takes on a new role or from the time a team or project starts up, but you can gain useful information even if you begin taking readings after an effort is well under way.

Find the average rating by adding the item ratings and dividing by 6. Plot the average rating each month on a chart like the one above, and you'll have an easy way to see when the individual, team, or project rises above the noise-value line and whether they stay above it. Ratings greater than 3.0 fall above the line; ratings lower than 3.0 fall below the line.

Time/Value Assessment

Scale: 1 = to a very small extent; 5 = to a very great extent

Assessment for an Individual Employee or Associate

People seek out this person to collaborate with on tasks or projects.   1   2   3   4   5

People consider this person knowledgeable in his or her area of responsibility.   1   2   3   4   5

This person stays focused on goals, avoiding distractions and
unnecessary work.   1   2   3   4   5

This person helps tasks and projects get accomplished with
high quality.   1   2   3   4   5

This person helps tasks and projects get accomplished
quickly.   1   2   3   4   5

When people need to solve a difficult problem, they go
to this person for advice.   1   2   3   4   5

Average rating: _____
Plot the average rating monthly on a noise-value chart (see figure 7-1).

Assessment for a Team, Task Force, or Work Group

This team executes on their decisions and assignments.
                                                     1   2   3   4   5

This team works together smoothly, avoiding unproductive
conflict.   1   2   3   4   5

People outside this team seek them out to collaborate
with.   1   2   3   4   5

This team stays focused on their goals, avoiding distractions
and unnecessary work.   1   2   3   4   5

The team members are comfortable raising difficult questions
and being open with one another.   1   2   3   4   5

This team gets strong buy-in from stakeholders to their
decisions and deliverables.   1   2   3   4   5

Average rating:_____
Plot the average rating monthly on a noise-value chart (see figure 7-1).

Assessment for a Project or Initiative

The project has goals that are clear and compelling to the core participants.   1 2 3 4 5

The project is on schedule, meeting the milestones that were set.   1 2 3 4 5

The core project team is working together smoothly, avoiding unproductive conflict.   1 2 3 4 5

People throughout the organization are eager to see the interim outputs of the project.   1 2 3 4 5

The leader of the project is giving it time, focus, and energy.   1 2 3 4 5

The core project team is adjusting to changes of plan and overcoming obstacles.   1 2 3 4 5

Average rating: _____

Plot the average rating monthly on a noise-value chart (see figure 7-1).

The Team Survey: Are Your People Clear, Unified, and Agile?

This short survey is designed to be filled out by the employees or team members who are involved in executing a strategy, initiative, or project that you are leading. In chapter 2 we presented the Strategic Speedometer, which is designed to be an assessment of clarity, unity, and agility that you complete yourself. This Team Survey, in contrast, gathers information from those you lead about how *they* perceive levels of clarity, unity, and agility within an initiative. We strongly recommend that you use this tool to supplement, and perhaps correct, your own perceptions. After all, if you want to know how you're doing on people factors, the best way to find out is to ask the people.

Feel free to reproduce this survey and hand it out. It takes about ten minutes to complete. You can hand it out as a paper questionnaire; or you can use it more formally, with anonymous responses, by loading it into an online survey tool; or you can use it very informally, in conversations with individuals. You can use it at any point in an initiative, or at multiple points.

The survey will give you:

- A sense of how you are doing on creating clarity, unity, and agility with respect to the strategy, initiative, or project

- Awareness of what you have been doing right and should do more of

- Ideas for what you might do differently in order to get better results

Team Survey

Dear _____,

We would like your opinion on the following initiative (strategy, project, task force):

_____.

With respect to this initiative:

1. Do you know where we're going and why?

No   Yes

If you answered No: What would need to happen for you to answer Yes to this question?

If you answered Yes: What has the initiative leader(s) done so far to enable you to answer Yes?

2. Are you committed to working with all the other people involved in order to get there?

No   Yes

> *If you answered No:* What would need to happen for you to answer Yes to this question?

> *If you answered Yes:* What has the initiative leader(s) done so far to enable you to answer Yes?

3. Are you willing to suggest and try many different ways to get there?

No   Yes

> *If you answered No:* What would need to happen for you to answer Yes to this question?

> *If you answered Yes:* What has the initiative leader(s) done so far to enable you to answer Yes?

The Leadership Profile: What's Slowing You Down?

This tool helps you diagnose your organization or business unit's strengths and weaknesses from the standpoint of the four leadership practices. We call the strengths *lift* and the weaknesses *drag*. Pinpointing the areas of drag and lift in your organization is an important step in accelerating execution. Once you and other leaders identify these areas, you'll know more about where you should all be focusing your efforts.

Each of the twenty-five items has a 5-point rating scale. The more an item contributes to lift, the higher the rating. For each item, circle the rating you think best reflects the circumstances in your organization and the things leaders are doing. Feel free to use half-steps (1.5, 2.5, etc.) if you prefer.

As you complete the profile, you can think either of a specific strategic initiative (initiative execution) or of your organization in general (everyday execution). If you're thinking of a specific initiative, then *leaders* means all the leaders and managers who are responsible for executing on that initiative. If you are thinking generally about your business unit, then *leaders* means the leaders and managers within that business unit. Similarly, *team members* means either the people executing on a specific initiative or all the members of your business unit. Your *business unit* is whatever part of the organization you lead—whether a function, division, department, or team.

Leadership Profile

Scale: 1 = to a very small extent; 5 = to a very great extent

Affirming Strategies

1. Leaders in this business unit are aligned and committed to the success of organizational strategies.　　1　2　3　4　5

2. Leaders in this business unit react quickly to changes in the business environment.　　1　2　3　4　5

3. When thinking about important decisions that affect the future, leaders' ideas are usually creative and innovative.　　1　2　3　4　5

4. Leaders demonstrate the ability to learn and improve continuously.　　1　2　3　4　5

5. Leaders are flexible about sharing and switching responsibilities to make things easier for each other.　　1　2　3　4　5

6. Leaders engage the business unit in frequent, effective communication about the strategy and its execution.　　1　2　3　4　5

- Average score: Sum items 1 through 6 and divide by 6: ____

- Lift-to-drag comparison: The number of lift items (with ratings equal to or greater than 4.0) minus the number of drag items (with ratings equal to or less than 2.0): ____

Driving Initiatives

For a specific initiative *or* for initiatives and projects in general:

7. Leaders ensure that teams have a high level of ability, the motivation, and the specific skills necessary to execute initiatives successfully.   1 2 3 4 5

8. Teams have clearly defined, appropriate, and measurable goals and milestones for executing initiatives.   1 2 3 4 5

9. Leaders continuously check progress against plans and make course corrections as required.   1 2 3 4 5

10. Leaders help their people understand and describe what they must do differently in their jobs in order to help strategies succeed.   1 2 3 4 5

11. The standard workload of people whose work is affected by large initiatives tends to be moderate and manageable.   1 2 3 4 5

12. Strategic initiatives are highly consistent with and support or enhance the organization's culture.   1 2 3 4 5

13. Leaders work to gain enthusiastic support for initiatives from the people affected by them.   1 2 3 4 5

- Average score: Sum items 7 through 13 and divide by 7: ____

- Lift-to-drag comparison: The number of lift items (with ratings equal to or greater than 4.0) minus the number of drag items (with ratings equal to or less than 2.0): ____

Managing Climate

14. Leaders work to ensure that team members have a clear understanding of the business unit's goals and objectives.   1 2 3 4 5

15. Leaders discuss what is expected of the business unit on a regular basis to ensure that everyone is informed and committed.   1 2 3 4 5

16. In our business unit, leaders set very high standards for performance.

    1 2 3 4 5

17. Leaders structure team members' work in a way that allows them to control how they do it.

    1 2 3 4 5

18. Good performance is recognized quickly in this business unit.

    1 2 3 4 5

19. In this business unit, colleagues enjoy working together.   1 2 3 4 5

- Average score: Sum items 14 through 19 and divide by 6:

  _____

- Lift-to-drag comparison: The number of lift items (with ratings equal to or greater than 4.0) minus the number of drag items (with ratings equal to or less than 2.0): _____

Cultivating Experience

20. Despite the workload, leaders allow people the time to review how the work is going.

    1 2 3 4 5

21. We experiment frequently with new ways of doing things in this business unit.

    1 2 3 4 5

22. Leaders help their teams capture and communicate lessons learned from their work.

    1 2 3 4 5

23. Even experienced employees in this business unit get training when new initiatives are launched.

    1 2 3 4 5

24. Leaders' number-one job is to develop their employees.   1 2 3 4 5

25. In this business unit, learning is treated as an important part of the work.

    1 2 3 4 5

- Average score: Sum items 20 through 25 and divide by 6:

  _____

- Lift-to-drag comparison: The number of lift items (with ratings equal to or greater than 4.0) minus the number of drag items (with ratings equal to or less than 2.0): _____

Leadership Profile Totals

- Your total average score: Sum of the four average scores divided by 4: ____

- Your total lift-to-drag comparison: The total number of lift items (with ratings equal to or greater than 4.0) minus the total number of drag items (with ratings equal to or less than 2.0): ____

Interpreting the Profile

Now that you've completed the Leadership Profile and calculated the averages, what do the numbers mean? As a general guide, assume the following:

- Items with ratings of 2.0 or less and sections that average 2.0 or less are *drag areas* that should be given attention. These areas are putting your organization at risk and represent opportunities for leaders to do better.

- Items or sections that average 4.0 or greater are *lift areas* and should be amplified. These are areas in which leaders perform relatively well and that are supporting strategic speed. You should make the most of these lift areas.

- Areas where the lift-to-drag comparison (the number of lift items minus the number of drag items) is less than zero are *problem areas*. Here, the potential drag outweighs the potential lift. A total lift-to-drag comparison of less than –5 is cause for serious concern.

To do a preliminary analysis of your Leadership Profile, follow these steps:

1. Find the drag areas (sections with an average score of 2.0 or less) and problem areas (sections where the lift-to-drag comparison is less than zero).

2. Look at the items within those drag and problem areas to
   see what might be causing the most drag. What things are
   happening in the organization to cause these low ratings?
   What are leaders doing or not doing?

3. Look across the assessment for lift areas (sections with an
   average score of 4.0 or greater), to see what strengths you
   might be able to leverage. How could these strengths be
   used to mitigate the problem areas?

The Speed Matrix: What Are Your Top Priorities for Action?

The next step in achieving strategic speed is determining some specific actions to take. You can't focus everywhere, so it's important to
pick just a few actions that you can be sure will give speed a boost
in your organization.

The Team Survey and the Leadership Profile gave you a sense
of your problem areas: the things that are slowing you down. You
can augment this data with the results of the Strategic Speedometer assessment from chapter 2 (which gave a sense of how well your
organization is doing on clarity, unity, and agility) and the results of
the quick assessments at the end of chapters 3 through 6 (which
told you how you personally are doing on each of the four leadership practices).

Armed with this information, you can now use the Speed Matrix
(see figure 7-2) to help you select a few actions that will have
the greatest impact on strategic speed in your business unit. For
example:

- If you need to boost clarity in your team, focus on the
  actions in the Clarity column.

FIGURE 7-2

Speed Matrix

HAVE YOU AND YOUR LEADERS FOCUSED ON THESE ACTIONS . . .

		If you need to increase . . .		
		Clarity	**Unity**	**Agility**
If you need to improve on . . .	**Affirming strategies**	1. Communicate the strategic direction or intent, the reasons for it, and people's role in supporting it	5. Seek each person's buy-in and ask for their commitment to making the strategy work	9. Educate people on external and internal business conditions and their implications for decisions
	Driving initiatives	2. Define and communicate specific objectives, roles, and action plans for executing the strategy	6. Coach people so they can see exactly how their job, skills, and behaviors contribute to the success of the whole	10. Stay involved in important initiatives and projects and help people make continuous course corrections
	Managing climate	3. Arrange frequent opportunities for dialogue about the organization's strategy and people's role in it	7. Encourage, model, and reward cross-boundary collaboration and teamwork	11. Give people greater control and flexibility in making decisions and pursuing objectives
	Cultivating experience	4. Create time and settings for people to reflect on their progress and obstacles in achieving goals	8. Provide each person with opportunities to offer insights and contribute to team knowledge	12. Implement practices that help people learn from experience and apply the lessons to emerging problems

- If you and leaders in your business unit need to improve on driving initiatives, focus on the actions in the Driving Initiatives row.

- If you have pinpointed, say, agility and affirming strategies as two areas where you need help, focus on action 9; if unity and managing climate are your key issues, focus on action 7; and so on.

Of course, the twelve actions in the Speed Matrix are not the only things you can do; there are many more tips and ideas contained within this book that you may want to consider. Ultimately, it's up to you as a leader to exercise your judgment in deciding which approaches to use and what to emphasize. These actions, however, are the ones that our research suggests will have the strongest positive effect on strategic speed.

The Future of Speed

F YOU'RE A BABY boomer or a Gen-X'er, you remember business in the 1980s and 1990s. Back then, we were awash in an alphabet soup of new management and technology tools: TQM, CRM, ERP, SFA, LMS—and more.[1] Business process reengineering (BPR) was godfather to all these tools, and all reflected the hope that streamlined processes and better technology would make things happen faster in organizations. It was a hope based on a mechanistic view of business: one that sees the organization fundamentally as a machine that can be designed in advance to deal smoothly and rapidly with any situation it encounters. This era represented "first-generation speed."

Today, some leaders still focus most of their attention on first-generation-speed practices and—like Jim Van Zoren, our misguided IT executive from the prologue—find their efforts going nowhere fast. They've spent years working with process consultants, automating supply chains, installing sophisticated software, and bestowing a mobile device on every employee—only to find themselves still groaning after many a meeting, "Why do things take forever to get done around here?!"

Other leaders, however, are practicing "second-generation speed" (a term coined by Christopher Meyer, former head of Ernst & Young's Center for Business Innovation).[2] If the first generation of speed was about achieving efficiency through process reengineering, lean manufacturing, and automation, the second generation of speed is about building on those concepts and adding a focus on *people*. Fast pace and efficient processes are enough when the road is straight, the obstacles are few, and the sole challenge is to drive quickly from A to B. But when the terrain is more complex than that (and when is it not?), your strategies and plans will live or die based on how your people understand them and what they choose to do with them. To achieve second-generation speed—*strategic speed*—leaders must do a masterful job both of optimizing processes and of mobilizing groups of human beings.

This book has been all about second-generation speed and how to achieve it. What comes next?

The third generation of speed, which we're already seeing come to life in some forward-thinking organizations, will build on the previous two. We've described in these pages how leaders look down, up, and across—to their employees, managers, and peers—as they seek to mobilize people and accelerate execution. The third generation of speed will find them looking *outward* as well, to their customers.

This book presents many cases of leaders of customer-facing teams working to reduce response times, shorten sales cycles, accelerate on-boarding, increase the value provided to clients, and the like. All these are impressive examples of strategic speed. But some organizations today are taking it one step further: *they're helping their customers speed up, too.* We expect this trend to grow. As leaders become more and more adept at building clarity, unity, and agility within their own firm, they'll begin to find ways to build clarity, unity, and agility in the customer's office, plant, or home. They'll find ways to influence and measure time to value and value over time not only for their own team or company, but for the individuals and companies who buy their products and services. People in customer-facing roles—the service providers, salespeople, technicians, and consultants who are on the front lines—will become more skilled at driving speed for their customers and clients.

One well-known example of third-generation speed is when Jeff Immelt, CEO of General Electric, began sharing GE's Six Sigma expertise with customers at no charge. But you don't have to be a CEO, or even a manager, to begin helping your customers move faster. We'll end with a brief story about a salesperson in Mumbai, India, who has succeeded in creating strategic speed for his customers.

As Vittorio Colao was settling into his chief executive role and planning to make speed a cornerstone for Vodafone Group Plc, he probably wasn't aware that at that moment, thousands of miles away in India, an IBM sales rep named Vivek Gupta was having similar thoughts.[3] Gupta, one of IBM's top salespeople in that part of the world, sold complex solutions to telecom companies—from call-center setups to sophisticated research services to huge customized billing systems. (Gupta could easily have been the lead salesperson from Worldwide Technology who closed the outsourcing deal with Jim Van Zoren.) Vodafone Essar, a subsidiary of Vodafone Group based in Mumbai, was one of Gupta's top prospects, but the managing director of Vodafone Essar was happy with his existing supplier relationships and had told Gupta he didn't intend to do any business with IBM.

Gupta was undaunted. He knew India was the fastest-growing mobile phone market in the world and that, as *Fortune* magazine reports, "small, inexperienced startups were battling for market share, and speed was everything." For telecom firms, "spending months or years hammering out back-office systems could spell the difference between dominating the industry and being an also-ran."[4] Gupta was confident that, from his position as sales professional and technology adviser, he could help his telecom customers increase their strategic speed. The suggestion he regularly put to them was that they could let IBM take care of all their operational functions—in effect "clearing the clutter" so that their people could focus sharply on more strategic issues.

After winning several deals to build or manage the back-office functions of some smaller telecoms in the region, Gupta began sowing seeds at Vodafone Essar. He knew the company saw speed as essential to its success. By starting out with a small order for laptops, he was able to get in the door and gradually make the business case for a similar kind of partnership: IBM would handle all of Vodafone's operational activities, from call centers to finances, thereby freeing Vodafone to focus on strategy and marketing. By making it clear how he could help the company accelerate execution in a marketplace where speed was everything, Gupta won over the managing director and ultimately closed a five-year, $600 million contract.

Whether it's a service center in Los Angeles that delivers parts sooner than promised 90 percent of the time, a consultant in London who teaches a CEO how to communicate more effectively about a strategic initiative, or a sales rep in Mumbai with a vision for speeding up an entire industry, we'll soon see more situations where fast companies are helping their customers move fast. When customers who need to accelerate execution call you first, you'll know you've achieved third-generation speed.

The Forum Corporation
and Economist Intelligence Unit
Global Speed Survey

I N THE COURSE of this study, we surveyed 343 respondents in 339 companies that represented a range of industries and geographies. About half (48 percent) were C-suite executives or board members and the rest were mostly senior managers with a broad view of their business. The sample comprised 50 percent relatively small companies (less than $500 million in annual revenue) and 40 percent large companies (over $1 billion), with the remaining 10 percent falling in between. The sample was balanced in terms of business strategies of customer intimacy (33 percent), operational excellence (33 percent), and product leadership (29 percent).

The Findings

The most important conclusions we drew from the survey are described below.

Speed Is Critical Everywhere

Nearly 90 percent of the 343 survey respondents agreed that speed of strategy execution is critical to their business. This finding confirms our expectation that executives view speed as critical to most companies today. Speed was rated as critical regardless of industry, size, geographic location, or business strategy.

Speed Correlates with Business Results

When we asked respondents to rate their company's overall speed of strategy execution relative to others in their industry, 42 percent described their company as "faster" or "much faster." For the 121 publicly held companies in the sample, we then compared the business performance during the previous three years of these faster/much faster companies with those rated slower. The faster companies had an average of 40 percent higher sales growth and 52 percent higher operating profit than their slower peer companies.

Speed Gaps Are Widespread

Respondents in most companies rated their company's speed of strategy execution as low relative to its importance. As with opinions about speed's criticality, we found these speed gaps (the gap between importance and current speed) across the globe and regardless of company characteristics.[1]

Execution Is Where the Slowdown Begins

We asked respondents to rank order the efficiency of their company in terms of six phases of strategic action: identifying an issue or opportunity, deciding to take action, creating a plan, executing the plan, assessing the result, and taking corrective action. Regardless of how fast or slow each company was, each rated its efficiency as greater in the upfront steps of identifying opportunities, planning,

FIGURE A-1

Execution is where the slowdown begins

Where is your company most efficient?
(rank order 1 to 6; 1 = most efficient; 6 = least efficient)

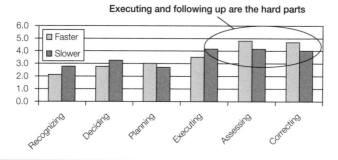

Executing and following up are the hard parts

and decision making; and weaker in executing the plan, assessing results, and making corrections (see figure A-1).

We compared the responses of executives in faster-moving companies with those in slower-moving companies to identify factors that might facilitate or inhibit speed. Three sets of factors distinguished faster and slower companies: the practices of their leaders; the way their project teams functioned; and characteristics of the companies in which the leaders and teams operate.

Companies That Execute with Speed Have Stronger Leadership

Leaders in faster companies were rated as significantly stronger on leadership practices, listed in descending order of the gap between faster and slower company ratings:[2]

- Identify and respond to threats and opportunities as they emerge (faster companies 68 percent/slower companies 21 percent)

- Execute strategic projects in a speedy and effective manner (61 percent/21 percent)

- Learn and improve from experience continuously (66 percent/33 percent)

- Maintain an organizational climate that drives employee engagement and high performance (57 percent/29 percent)

- Create a shared understanding of the business strategy (72 percent/27 percent)

The picture of the leader that emerges from these findings is one who is both externally and internally focused. That is, the leader is constantly scanning the external environment for threats and opportunities, and is also able to mobilize internal teams to respond. The leader takes time to make sure people understand the strategy, builds a climate that motivates people, is disciplined about execution, and helps teams learn and improve through experience.

Teams Operate Differently in Companies That Execute with Speed

We asked respondents to think about a successful initiative in their organization that required speed. We then asked them to choose from a set of paired statements the ones that best described the project teams that executed the initiative.

Teams in faster companies were described by respondents as:

- Taking time to capture lessons learned at the end of a project versus moving on to the next project without a debrief (faster companies 63 percent/slower companies 43 percent)

- Being flexible about switching responsibilities with each other versus focusing on their own responsibilities (55 percent/36 percent)

- Being comfortable discussing problems or disagreements versus keeping quiet (73 percent/60 percent)

- Having senior leaders who were closely aligned and committed to their success versus succeeding in spite of lack of alignment and commitment (83 percent/ 70 percent)

- Taking time to review and reflect versus focusing solely on getting the work done (75 percent/65 percent)

Given how important we have found leadership to be in driving speed, it is no surprise that teams that execute with speed also have leaders who are aligned with one another and committed to their teams' success. We believe leadership alignment facilitates speed by helping teams avoid false starts and redundant or competing efforts and ensuring that they get the direction and resources they need in order to move quickly.

We noticed a paradox in the team-factor findings. Many of the factors that are associated with speed require some slowing down: taking time to debrief projects, fostering open discussion and reflection, and trying out different roles versus taking a "heads down" approach to getting the work done. We believe that these teams ultimately achieve greater speed and effectiveness by slowing down at key moments to make sure everyone is clear and aligned on the strategy, resolve differences, explore new approaches, and discuss lessons learned. The findings suggest that achieving speed is sometimes a matter of "slowing down to speed up."

Companies That Move More Quickly See Things Differently

We asked respondents to select from a set of paired statements those that best described their company. Again, we found significant differences between companies rated as faster and those rated as slower. Respondents rated their companies as:

- Having a senior management team that bases important decisions on creative and innovative ideas versus the tried and true ones (faster companies 66 percent/slower companies 41 percent)

- Having management systems that work coherently to support their objectives versus having systems that cause people to work at cross-purposes on competing objectives (74 percent/50 percent)

- Creating innovative products and services versus fine-tuning existing ones (59 percent/37 percent)

- Defining success based on the ability to explore new technologies, products, services, and markets versus improving quality and lowering costs of existing products and services (68 percent/48 percent)

- Providing training and education even for experienced people when new initiatives are launched versus allowing no time for training (67 percent/51 percent)

The themes in the company factors echo those of the leadership and team factors. That is, companies that achieve speed have aligned and supportive leadership; they are open to new ideas and innovative solutions; and they take time to ensure that people are trained and prepared for their role in executing projects. In addition, they have management support systems, such as performance management systems and training and development, that facilitate speed by ensuring that goals are consistent with strategy.

The Cultural Aspects of Speed

OUR RESEARCH on strategic speed identified a set of people factors and leadership practices that can be applied across a broad range of cultures. We are aware, however, that cultural differences play a major role in how people perceive speed and take action to improve it. To better understand these differences, we consulted with noted expert David Eaton, cofounder of Aperian Global, a cross-cultural consulting firm. This section reflects his insights.

In human culture, unlike in physics, speed means different things to different people. Americans, for example, often see speed in a positive light—indeed, as good in its own right. Some U.S. businesspeople value speed more than quality. By comparison, people in most other cultures would value relationships first, quality second, and speed third.

Nevertheless, most businesspeople in most cultures do seek ways to accelerate execution in their organizations. It's simply important to recognize that people in different cultures face different challenges and beliefs with respect to speed. Americans may need to gain an appreciation of the factors—such as attitudes toward hierarchy, status, and risk—that affect perceptions of speed elsewhere in the world. And people in more risk-averse, hierarchical, status-conscious cultures may need to value these elements of their culture while simultaneously learning to make decisions and take action with greater strategic speed.

There's no easy answer to the question of how to increase strategic speed across multiple cultures, but two imperatives can help:

- First, understand how speed is viewed in different cultures.

- Second, provide people in the business community with tools and strategies that will increase *pace*, streamline *processes*, and—most important—enhance the *people* factors of clarity, unity, and agility.

Here's an overview of the most important factors affecting views on speed throughout the world.

Quality

Orientation toward quality is different in different cultures. In Germany, for instance, it's considered less professional or less impressive if a task isn't accomplished or a goal reached perfectly the first time. Thus the Germans would tend to do thoughtful research, acquire thorough data, and build multiple prototypes of a product before taking it to the demo stage, putting it on line, testing it, and launching it. This approach creates long lead times. Precisely because there's been so much group interaction on the data, however—the research, the background tasks, and all the checking and rechecking—most products will be launched without a hitch.

Compare this approach with what's common in California's Silicon Valley. Launching version 1.0 of a product means sending it to the marketplace as fast as possible. American consumers pay for that version because they want it first—the new iPhone, the new iTouch, the new BlackBerry, and so forth. The company calls this a beta test; early adopters try out the product, provide feedback, and then eagerly await—and pay for—version 2.0. And in a third example, many Asian cultures produce no "versions." Companies typically send one perfect product after another out the door. There are teams working constantly on new products to polish and send through the pipeline each year.

American culture thrives on change, risk, and innovation. But four-fifths of the people in the world would respond to this set of attitudes with a firm: "No way." If a product is touted as "new and improved," a typical response in many countries would be to ask, "Why wasn't it done right in the first place?" By comparison, if a company *doesn't* release an improved product for several years, the American consumer would wonder why there aren't any upgrades.

Relationships

Cultures throughout much of the world place primacy on relationships. Stepping on relationships to achieve speed—relationships that have existed for generations and are expected to last for generations—is asking for trouble. Disrupting the harmony (what the Japanese call the *wah*) of the situation is hard to forgive. Those from cultures that reverence elders would never do anything to destroy what the generations before them have created. People in Mexico, Saudi Arabia, Italy, or Korea would never jeopardize a relationship simply to increase speed; for Americans, however, speed can sometimes justify the means to attain it.

Hierarchy

In a hierarchical, risk-averse, group-oriented culture like the pre-dominant cultures of Japan and India, a definite order controls the decision-making process. All decisions made and actions taken require approval from a formal chain of command. In Japan, for example, every person has a *chop*—his or her signature or mark—and members of the team will put their chop in a vertical line on a proposal to signal their approval. When all team members at one level have added their chops, the proposal moves up to the next level. The result is a bottom-up decision-making process. This approach creates full buy-in. It also honors hierarchy and group orientation, and it disperses risk. The catch: it takes time. An initiative launched the Japanese way may take longer to rise above the noise-value line, but once there, its value over time is likely to stick.

Direct Versus Indirect Speech

Some cultures value more direct speech, while others put a premium on an indirect approach. Direct speech, for instance, allows the Dutch to spar and debate in order to produce some strong results along the way and, sometimes, to increase speed. As international companies raced to develop the first flat-screen TVs, for instance, new product introductions were faster at Philips than at Sony, in part because the Dutch leaders were able to say, "Okay, we've heard from everybody. Thanks very much. This is what we're going to do." By contrast, the "chop" system in Japan requires such comprehensive buy-in from the bottom up that by the time Sony reached the sign-off phase, it was a number of months behind Philips.

Individualism Versus Collectivism

Here's a story that shows how culture can affect concepts of speed. There were twenty children in a Japanese kindergarten classroom and twenty in an American kindergarten. The teachers in both classrooms received the same instructions: seat five children at each of four tables; put five sheets of paper and a bucket of crayons at the center of each table; and instruct the children to draw a spaceship. In the Japanese classroom, each child selected one crayon; then each table group pulled down one sheet of paper in front of one child naturally selected by the group, without talking; and then each group collaborated to design a single spaceship. They took their time. The leader had emerged—the oldest kid, biggest kid, most daring kid, or whatever—within a clear hierarchy. When the teacher told them that their time was up, each table group came forward with their heads bowed, presented their joint effort, and said, "We're sorry, teacher—we did the best we could." In the American classroom, each child grabbed some crayons, took his or her own sheet of paper, went off somewhere in the room, covered up the work-in-progress, drew his or her own spaceship, and soon came racing to the front of the room: "Teacher—I'm done, I'm done!" The clear assumption was that the first child who finished was the winner. In both the Japanese and the American classrooms, no one had said anything in advance about time.

What does the story tell us? A lot—including a lot about how early and intensely each of us learns not just about the nature of speed and execution, but also about who we are as individuals and group members as we go about our tasks. We would argue that the American children geared the spaceship assignment toward pace: they treated it purely as a race (of individuals) to the finish. The Japanese children provided an impressive example of unity—one of the people factors that increase speed—but we know that unity alone is not enough to create strategic speed. Perhaps this story helps us see that no single culture has a real handle (yet) on strategic speed, and that leaders will need to cultivate and blend the unique experiences and strengths of many cultures in order to achieve true strategic speed within their increasingly global organizations.

NOTES

Chapter One

1. The Forum Corporation, strategy execution research conducted in 2007 and 2008.

2. Michael C. Mankins and Richard Steele, "Closing the Strategy-to-Performance Gap," *Harvard Business Review*, July–August 2005.

3. Alex Taylor III, "It's Clutch Time for Fritz Henderson and GM," *Fortune*, October 12, 2009.

4. Douglas P. Shuit, "GM Goes Fast," *Workforce Management*, http://www.workforce.com, March 2004.

5. J. Richard Hackman and Diana Coutu, "Why Teams Don't Work," *Harvard Business Review*, May 2009.

Chapter Two

1. Michael H. Hugos, *Business Agility: Sustainable Prosperity in a Relentlessly Competitive World* (Hoboken, NJ: Wiley, 2009).

2. Saj-nicole Joni, "Lehman's Problem? Too Much Alignment," September 18, 2009, http://blogs.harvardbusiness.org/hbr/hbr-now/2009/09/lehmans-problem-too-much-align.html.

3. Note that we combined two of the survey items, "Identify and respond to threats and opportunities as they emerge" and "Learn and improve from experience continuously" into one leadership practice, "cultivating experience."

Chapter Three

1. Donald C. Hambrick and James W. Fredrickson, "Are You Sure You Have a Strategy?" *Academy of Management Executive* 15, no. 4 (1993): 48–59.

2. Paul C. Nutt, "Leverage, Resistance, and the Success of Implementation Approaches," *Journal of Management Studies* 35, no. 2 (March 1998): 213–240.

3. Ibid.

4. W. Chan Kim and Renée Mauborgne, *Blue Ocean Strategy: How to Create Uncontested Market Space and Make the Competition Irrelevant* (Boston: Harvard Business School Press, 2005).

Chapter Four

1. Larry Bossidy and Ram Charan, *Execution: The Discipline of Getting Things Done* (NY: Crown Business Books, 2002).

2. Michael C. Mankins and Richard Steele, "Closing the Strategy-to-Performance Gap," *Harvard Business Review*, July–August 2005.

Chapter Five

1. George H. Litwin and Robert A. Stringer, Jr., *Motivation and Organizational Climate* (Boston: Division of Research, Graduate School of Business Administration, Harvard University, 1968).

2. Ibid.

3. Gary S. Hansen and Birger Wernerfelt, "Determinants of Firm Performance: The Relative Importance of Economic and Organizational Factors," *Strategic Management Journal* 10, no. 5 (September 1989): 399–411.

4. See, for example, Nancy R. Lockwood, "Leveraging Employee Engagement for Competitive Advantage: HR's Strategic Role," *HR Magazine*, March 2007, 1–11.

5. Paul T. P. Wong, "The Positive Psychology of 'Climate Management,'" www.meaning.ca/articles/presidents_column/climate_management.html.

6. Daniel Goleman, "Leadership That Gets Results," *Harvard Business Review*, March–April 2000, 78–90.

7. The Forum Corporation, "How Sales Forces Sustain Competitive Advantage," research report (Boston, 2004).

8. Joshua Freedman, "Case Study: Emotional Intelligence at the Sheraton Studio City Hotel," white paper, Six Seconds Institute for Organizational Performance (www.sixseconds.com), 2003.

9. George H. Litwin and John J. Bray, "Customer Climate: The Key to Long-Term Retention" The Climate Guild, white paper (Boston: August 2003).

10. Ibid.

11. See, for example, The Forum Corporation, *Managing the Customer Experience*, 2002; Robert A. Stringer, *Leadership and Organizational Climate: The Cloud Chamber Effect* (Upper Saddle River, NJ: Prentice Hall, 2002); Litwin and Bray, "Customer Climate."

12. See, for example, Alfie Kohn, *Punished by Rewards: The Trouble with Gold Stars, Incentive Plans, A's, Praise, and Other Bribes* (Boston: Houghton Mifflin, 1999).

13. Gerard Seijts and Dan Crim, "What Engages Employees the Most, or the Ten C's of Employee Engagement," *Ivey Business Journal* (March–April 2006).

Chapter Six

1. See, for example, Robert W. Eichinger and Michael M. Lombardo, *The Leadership Machine: Architecture to Develop Leaders for Any Future* (3rd ed.) (Minneapolis: Lominger Limited, Inc., 2006).

2. Sarah Jane Gilbert, "Q&A with Amy C. Edmonson," *Harvard Business School Working Knowledge*, April 23, 2007, http://www.hbswk.hbs.edu.

3. K. Anders Ericsson, Ralf Th. Krampe, and Clemens Tesch-Romer, "The Role of Deliberate Practice in the Acquisition of Expert Performance," *Psychological Review* 100, no. 3, (1993): 363–406; Geoff Colvin, "Why Talent Is Overrated," *Fortune*, October 27, 2008; Malcolm Gladwell, *Outliers: The Story of Success* (New York: Little, Brown and Co., 2008).

4. Ericsson, Krampe, and Tesch-Romer, "The Role of Deliberate Practice in the Acquisition of Expert Performance."

5. Marilyn Darling, Charles Parry, and Joseph Moore, "Learning in the Thick of It," *Harvard Business Review*, July–August 2005, 84–92.

6. Ibid.

7. Mohan Nair, *Essentials of Balanced Scorecard* (Hoboken, NJ: John Wiley & Sons, 2004).

Epilogue

1. Total quality management, customer relationship management, enterprise resource planning, sales force automation, and learning management systems, respectively.

2. Deone M. Zell, Alan M. Glassman, Shari Duron, "Strategic Management in Turbulent Times," *Organizational Dynamics*, January 2007, 99.

3. Jessi Hempel, "IBM's All-Star Salesman," *Fortune*, September 26, 2008.

4. Ibid.

Appendix A

1. The ratings of speed were subjective; however, they correlated with company performance (higher sales growth and higher operating profit, as described above).

2. All gaps were statistically significant at $p < .01$.

INDEX

ABOUT THE AUTHORS

Jocelyn R. Davis is Executive Vice President, Research and Development, at The Forum Corporation. Her global team is responsible for advancing Forum's expertise and intellectual property in four areas: leadership, sales and customer experience, strategy execution, and workplace learning. She has consulted to companies in a range of industries and is the author of numerous research reports, training courses, and articles. Jocelyn received a BA with high honors from Swarthmore College and an MA from the University of Pittsburgh. She lives in Santa Fe, New Mexico, with her husband, Matt, and daughter, Emily.

As Director of Research and executive consultant, *Henry M. Frechette, Jr.* has led The Forum Corporation's research program for the past five years, studying leadership practices, learning, organizational climate, and strategic speed. His most recent research involves testing ways to increase the impact of learning on business results. As a consultant, he has worked all over the world, guiding senior leadership teams and helping them create and implement their strategy initiatives. He holds a PhD in industrial and organizational psychology from the University of Tennessee. He has six children and lives in Reading, Massachusetts, with his wife, Judy.

Edwin H. Boswell is President and CEO of The Forum Corporation. For over two decades, he has helped organizations around the globe execute their most important strategic initiatives through their people in industries as diverse as pharmaceuticals, financial services, chemicals, energy, and professional services. Before joining Forum, Ed worked as an organizational change consultant for Human Systems and as an account executive for IBM. He earned his BA from the University of Texas at Austin and his PhD from the University of Pennsylvania. He and his wife, Lynne, live in Wellesley, Massachusetts, and have three children.

Contact the authors and learn more about The Forum Corporation at www.forum.com.